CREATIVE PLANTING IDEAS

RECIPES FOR GREAT GARDENS

BY CAROLINE GUNTER

The Australian Women's Weekly garden guides

C O N T

E N T S

CREATIVE PLANTING IDEAS

*P*ictured here is a collection of gardens growing in various climates and conditions. The information with each garden gives directions on how to achieve this look, with details of seasons, soil preparation and the plants to replicate it almost exactly — nature very gently will make her own variations. As far as is possible alternative plants and treatments are suggested so that something similar can be achieved in different growing conditions.

But it is also hoped that the 'creative' part of the title can be called into play, and that these gardens will inspire you to create a new garden or simply to add snippets from some of them to your existing display. Perhaps there will be plants you're not familiar with, colour combinations or techniques you haven't previously used or unusual designs that will give you ideas to help solve the ever-present problem of what to put where in your garden.

The aim is to make it achievable for you, so there are instructions for soil preparation, including fertilising and mulching, advice on placement and maintenance of each plant, conservative watering regimes and information on achieving a harmonious effect throughout the year.

Plants can survive if you just shove them into the ground. Roots will move through the air spaces in the soil to search out water. They will absorb mineral elements from the soil dissolved in the water and, with sunlight, will convert these to new cells for growth of stems, leaves, flowers and seed.

They must have some of all the above: soil, air, water, minerals and sunlight to survive. Some plants have modified their need for some of these elements, enabling them to thrive in less than perfect conditions, becoming drought-tolerant, or frost-tolerant or able to live in water, for example. Where relevant, information is given about such characteristics so those plants can be utilised in solving planting problems in your garden.

ABOVE: It looks like a pretty wilderness, but it's actually a well planned and very well maintained cottage garden. Walking through it is a delight with its various leaf and flower shapes and its delicious scents. Gardens like this that look as if they happened quite by accident are often the ones that have been most well tended.

However plants merely surviving don't look their best. Most gardeners try to create the right conditions for plants to look really good, flowering, growing and fruiting as designed. The techniques that are mentioned in this book are to help in developing the right conditions for optimum growth and delightful effects. It's hoped experienced gardeners may find new insights and beginners all the help they need to create the difference between a just surviving garden and a great garden. ❧

~ THE SOIL

Soil is a precious compilation of decomposed rock particles, organic matter and organisms, that has collected over many years, and been modified by wind, water and volcanic activity. The resultant soil type is dependent on these factors, making it clay, loam or sand. Squeeze a handful of moist soil into a ball. If it forms a sticky ball it is clay; if it crumbles apart it is loam; and if it won't even hold together it is sand. There are often differing layers of soil types with rock or hard subsoil underneath.

SLOW DRAINING SOIL is usually clay, the fine grained particles sticky and slippery when wet, and hard clumped together when dry. If it's had a lot of foot traffic, heavy machinery or been excavated and dumped as so often happens on building sites, it will be compacted together and there will be no spaces for air or water to move through. Gypsum will break up the clumps. It is available under a number of brand names with instructions on the packet on how to apply. A generous 10cm to 15cm layer of topsoil, manure, garden or mushroom compost or mulch (or a combination of any two or three) spread over the gypsum will prepare the soil for planting. Dig only into the added top layer, not into the clay, or pooling will result and plant roots will drown. Three months later the top surface can be dug into the now open clay and a new mulch added to the surface. Continually repeating this process adds organic matter to the clay, allowing air and moisture to move through it, and the rich nutrient supply stored around the clay particles to be available to the plants. Gypsum can be used under a thick newspaper mulch which is useful in suppressing weeds and grasses, and the mulch layer placed over this. Don't dig clay soil when it is really wet as each spadeful will become a solid clump. Just-moist conditions will allow you to break up the lumps.

FAST DRAINING SOIL is usually associated with sandy or gravelly soils, the soil particles are large and air and water move freely through. The addition of the same mulches and composts spread over the top will slow down water loss and add nutrients so essential for plant growth. Always ensure that manure and compost dug into soil has been exposed to the air for at least two weeks and is well broken down otherwise anaerobic breakdown produces undesirable gases and fungal diseases. Sandy soils need frequent addition of manure and fertiliser to maintain plant growth; it should be applied three or four times a year.

LOAMS also benefit from additions of organic material as fertiliser and mulch. Their draining speed can be slowed by using thick layers of fine mulch and increased by using larger-particled matter.

~ MULCH

Mulch is a layer of organic material that is spread over the soil and around plants to enrich the soil, reduce weed growth, reduce water loss and protect roots from excessive heat and frost.

GARDEN COMPOST can be made at home by mounding together kitchen vegetable waste, garden trimmings, weeds, vacuum cleaner contents, leaves and grass clippings. In fact anything that was once alive. Meat products, dog waste and weed bulbs are not usually added; they can lead to fly invasion, risk of infection and regrowth respectively. Manure and blood and bone are good additions. Lime can help keep things sweet and speed up breakdown, but don't use this compost around lime-hating plants like camellias and azaleas.

SPENT MUSHROOM COMPOST is a useful mulch but can be too limey (alkaline) for some plants. It is available from nurseries and mushroom growers.

COMMERCIAL MULCHES like wood chips, bark chips and leaf mulch are available from nurseries and landscape suppliers. For large areas it is best bought in bulk, but it is available bagged as well, and this quantity may be all you need. To make leaf mulch at home it is best to pile and compost them for a couple of months before spreading as the composting process will draw nitrogen from the garden to aid their breakdown.

STRAW AND HAY make excellent mulches, but they may introduce field weeds to the garden. They are also good frost protectors when placed around delicate plants and tree trunks. Nitrogen-rich lucerne hay or pea straw are preferred by many gardeners.

MANURES from cows, chickens, sheep and horses are used as mulches and soil conditioners because of the large quantity of organic matter they contain. They also contain plant nutrients (see Fertilisers below). Spread manure thickly over a resting bed in winter, avoiding close contact with any plants. Dig it in come spring planting time. Composted manures have lost the burning strength of their nutrients and can be spread as mulch over the soil around plants at any time.

GRAVEL AND PEBBLES can be used as moisture- and weed-controlling mulches but are not usually dug into the soil.

ABOVE: This lovely spring garden has two varieties of Tritonia *that were planted in clusters many years ago. Suiting this environment they have spread generously. Don't mow after first leaves show through in autumn. Let them yellow before mowing again, to ensure healthy productive bulbs.*

They provide a continuous supply of fertiliser, come with a variety of lengths of efficacy: three, six or twelve months, and can be positioned around a single needy specimen or in potted plants.

PH VALUE Another feature of soil that will determine what will survive or fail in your garden is its pH value — whether it is acid or alkaline. pH for growing most cultivated plants needs to be just slightly acid, but some plants have a preference for alkalinity. Use a pH tester or have the soil tested at your local nursery. Agricultural lime or dolomite will neutralise excess acidity, and sulphate of iron or sulphate of ammonia will reduce alkalinity. Do not use more than the rates recommended.

～ FERTILISERS

ORGANIC FERTILISERS are usually smelly as they consist of decomposed organic matter. These include such treasures as animal manures, fish emulsions, blood and bone, pelleted poultry manure, compost and leaf mulch. They are what would be added to the soil by nature in a wild garden. Check that neighbours are not planning an outdoor event before airing manure piles. Once composted in the air the manure can be dug in or covered over with mulch to reduce the aroma. When applied as liquid manure, made by soaking a quarter of a bucket of manure in water and diluting the liquid to weak tea strength before applying directly onto the plants, the effect on the air is short lived but significantly observable on the plant.

CHEMICAL FERTILISERS are marketed with their specific proportions of ingredients displayed on the package. Nitrogen (N) is essential for the growth of leaf and stem. Where the aim is leafy growth in plants like spinach,

lettuce, ferns and hostas, nitrogen is essential. Extra supplies will produce a more robust plant. Phosphorus (P) assists in root, stem and bud growth. Potassium (K) regulates and aids photosynthesis and disease resistance. Calcium, magnesium and sulphur are also used by plants, as are numerous trace elements. When any of these become unavailable or in overdose proportions, introduced plants will suffer, so do not apply more than the recommended quantity. The first signs are usually discolouration of the leaves or malformations. If problems arise refer to books, take a leaf to your nursery or send a photo with an explanation to the botanic garden in your area.

COMPLETE FERTILISER will provide a mix of all the essential and minor elements needed for plant growth. It is useful in areas of massed planting.

SLOW RELEASE FERTILISERS are pellets of complete fertiliser wrapped in a porous polymer coating which will release nutrients into the soil with each watering.

～ WATERING

Water is such a precious resource in most areas of the world, it should be treated with respect. Mulching to reduce water loss, placing of water-demanding plants in groups or in slow draining soil, and long slow waterings when needed are some ways to reduce the demand. Gardeners often fall in love with plants that need different conditions from the ones at hand and will want to grow water-hungry plants in dry conditions. It is possible to create appropriate micro-climates but it will always be a battle. It can be just as exciting a challenge to seek out plants that will give a similar effect to the plants you love, but will grow happily in your conditions without excessive demands on additional water. Observe what does well in neighbouring gardens or what your nursery can suggest to achieve the look you want. Where possible alternative plantings to heavy waterers have been listed should you want to try them.

∽ TRIMMING AND PRUNING

Trimming describes the light tidying pruning using scissors or fingernail nips on soft stems, rather than the heavier pruning that requires sharp secateurs to cut through woody stems. Some shrubs will not regrow from cuts to woody stems so look up information about the plant before doing anything too radical or check with your local nursery. Most perennials are cut back to ground level at the end of flowering, or when leaves yellow if they are tuber- or bulb-based. They may need an occasional trim or prune when they grow too leggy and lean on their neighbours. Shrubs are usually best controlled if pruned after flowering, so new growth can develop with buds for the next show. Damaged, dead or diseased pieces should be removed. Trimming off finished blooms keeps the plant looking tidy and encourages new flowering as the plant flowers to produce its seed. Drop trimmings as mulch where they can't be seen if they haven't fungal problems, or add them to the compost. Regular harvesting of flowers for vases or gifts is one of the pleasures of gardening, as beneficial to the plants as to the gardener. Roses with attractive hips, plants with feature seed cases, or seeds that are required for new stocks are exceptions to the trim it off routine.

TOPIARY-shaping needs extra care. When buying a plant that you wish to cut into shape, try to select one that has the beginnings of the form you're looking for. Lightly trim back each new stem as it protrudes beyond the established border edge or shape after each growth burst. Light regular trimming will prevent the development of woody protruding stems, and keep the plants bushy. When establishing a shape from small plants trim off half the new growth regularly to let the plant bush slowly into the intended shape. Always cut back to a leaf/stem junction so new growth can develop from that point.

∽ THE PLANTS

All the trees, shrubs, bulbs, perennials and annuals mentioned in this book should be available from your nursery, either from stocks there or ordered in. When purchasing or ordering plants, use the botanical name to avoid any confusion — common names differ from country to country and even from state to state. Take the book with you or write the names down if you are not familiar with them.

SEEDS can be purchased and raised in punnets or seedling trays or in the garden — follow the directions on the packet. They must be kept moist. Plant them out when their true leaves have developed, in prepared soil where the manure, if using, is well broken down to prevent "burning off" the seedlings. Don't plant out in very hot weather unless you can shade them well. Keep them moist until the roots become established. Many annuals will seed themselves and present you with volunteer seedlings, some from your stock, but others blown in the wind or donated by birds. If you do not recognise the plant, give it time to show itself before whisking it out as a weed. You will learn quickly which are the major invading weeds and getting them out early saves space, water, and nutrients for your plants. Usually some of the volunteers will have to be discarded and most probably some will have to be repositioned.

SEEDLINGS can be raised inside or under glass protection to get an early start in planting after winter. As long as they have been "hardened off" they can often be planted straight into the garden.

PRUNING

Above left: Prune just above a leaf junction on roses and all shrubs. Centre: Correct pruning angle. Right: Incorrect pruning angle — too high above bud.

To prune shrubs, cut out dead wood and crossing stems low down. Reduce top twiggy growth to encourage new bushiness.

Prune back woody perennials at end of their season or in early spring to encourage compact growth and abundant flowering stems.

Using scissors or designer pruning tools, regularly trim off all small shoots of topiary. Allow them to just extend outside the outline until final shape and size is reached.

❧ CUTTINGS

Some of the shrubby perennials like salvia, geranium, wallflower, carnations and gazania to name a few, and most shrubs, can be grown from cuttings. It's a very useful technique when you want a specific plant from a friend's garden or you'd like to increase or replace your own stock. Of course it takes time, so instant display is not possible this way, but it is less expensive and your specific plants are your reward. Cuttings, when planted in a pretty pot, can also be given as gifts or sold at fetes or other fund-raising efforts.

TAKING CUTTINGS There are ideal times in the growth cycle to get the best results, but keeping the potting mix or soil moist is the most important factor. The stem, no longer attached to the plant, must be able to draw up water to survive and develop its own roots. Ideally the stems used should have made their new growth and be just getting some strength to hold up. They should not be coming into flower as the plant's energy will go into flowering rather than forming roots. If necessary nip out the bud. Cut at a leaf node or leaf/stem junction, making cuttings about 10cm or 15cm long and remove the lower leaves so only two or three remain on the top. Make a hole in the potting mix with your finger or a stick and put the cutting in,

firming the mix around the stem. It's wise to position several cuttings in the pot at the same time as success is not always guaranteed. Keep the potting mix moist. When new leaves appear on the cuttings, transplant to individual larger pots, and plant them out when they get to the required size. Some wiry-stemmed shrubs make roots more easily from cuttings pulled from the stem with a "heel" of the old wood attached. Trim off ragged end and plant as above.

❧ DIVISIONS

Plants that grow into a clump — this includes perennials, spreading shrubs, bulbs, tubers and enlarged underground stems (rhizomes) can be dug up and divided during their dormant stage. Old decaying central sections are discarded, and new vigorous sections are repositioned. A larger clump makes more impact so unless you are moving them for aesthetic reasons, or to increase your supplies, only divide them every two or three years. Healthy roots and even shoots will ensure success but don't make the new clumps too small. Sharp secateurs or a knife will give clean cuts and a sharp spade may well be necessary to divide large clumps. It can be heavy work with old established clumps of agapanthus, clivea, red hot poker

and the like. Make sure you remove all traces of roots if moving the clump, as they will probably grow again.

BULBS that have grown into a congested clump are lifted when dormant. You may have to mark the position before the leaves die down. Break them into clumps of at least three or four bulbs for full impact when flowering, give them an airing in a cool atmosphere or provide them with an artificial winter as described for tulips below. They will acclimatise to the conditions in your garden and can remain growing into enormous clumps over time. Older bulbs will die but are replaced many times over by newer ones. Replant to a depth three times their height with composted manure or complete plant food mixed into the soil.

TULIPS must have a cold winter if they are to flower. An artificial cold winter can be provided by storing the bulbs for six to eight weeks in the crisper drawer of the refrigerator, properly labelled to avoid mistaken consumption, of course. Then they are planted into cold soil, in late autumn in cold climates and during winter where it is milder. They are not successful if the soil does not chill. Lift them after the leaves dry and store in a cool place if conditions are mild. If frosty, snowy winters are yours, tulips will not need this treatment.

STRIKING CUTTINGS

Select cuttings from healthy plants. Cut diagonally just above a leaf junction and remove excess leaves from the top.

Firm down the cuttings in good quality potting mix. Take more cuttings than you need to allow for failures.

Cover with a plastic bag, held up with stakes, to keep humidity in. Secure around rim with elastic band.

ABOVE: Here is an old-fashioned mixed garden border, well cared for and full of flowers. Regular cutting of blooms encourages more buds to grow. Pick them for vases or give bunches to friends and neighbours so they can share in your garden's beautiful bounty.

DAHLIAS need help in frosty conditions. Cut back the caney stems before they get too tatty-looking, and lift the clump of tubers before frosts start to chill the soil. Wash or shake off the soil, label the flower colours if necessary to get the right one in the right place when replanting, and hang them in an airy but not freezing place. Divide the clump by breaking off the tubers and ensuring there is some of last year's stem still attached. The growth eyes are at this end. When replanting in deeply dug, rich, well drained soil, position the eyes 8cm to 15cm below the surface. If it is a tall-growing type, put in a stake for individual tubers or at the centre of a group of three. You'll need these to tie stems to later, and it's much easier to position them before the plants get too big. If frost is not a problem, cut back canes, mulch, feed and reposition stakes as needed. Clumps can be lifted and divided as described every two or three years, to keep the plants healthy and provide them with a new patch of soil.

RHIZOMES, as seen on irises and cannas, are enlarged underground stems. It is best to divide them after flowering. Trim back stems or foliage, lift the plant with a fork, cut away dead or diseased pieces of the rhizome and replant the vigorous new sections with a growing tip and some roots attached. Plant irises shallowly so the tubers can bake in the sun.

∾ SAFETY

Accidents can occur with any activity and gardening can present quite a few, but most can be avoided. Take care with sharp implements, don't leave them lying casually around, especially sharp-end up, waiting to be trodden on. Stand them up between tasks and store them safely to protect them. Wear protective clothing against sun, plant, chemical spray and implement damage. That means head, eyes, arms, legs, feet and hands can and should be protected. The gardener will be a lot more productive and confident. When using chemical sprays on the garden, always wear a mask or wet scarf across your nose and mouth to prevent inhalation. Goggles are a very good idea too, not just to protect your eyes from chemical burns, but to prevent accidental scratches from sharp branches. Check scratches and wounds by cleaning away blood and apply antiseptic liquid or cream. Be aware of plants that will irritate skin, eyes, nose and breathing. Keep tetanus injections up to date. Don't take risks with insects and spiders or snakes. And protect the back by using safe lifting, digging and reaching techniques. Knee cushions or knee pads will protect when kneeling.

AN AUTUMN BORDER

The grand finale of the warmer seasons is seen here in this temperate garden's borders. Fine specimens of perennials in exuberant mixed colours are well maintained and controlled. Touches of white and grey break up the richness. This is a nursery border so is designed to display. From it you can select groupings, details or the whole scene for your garden.

Such a planting needs very well tended soil. Lavishly mulched with manure and blood and bone and rested during winter, it's then turned in and deeply dug in spring when planting begins. Complete plant food is added with each planting, and repeated in summer and autumn, to maintain the garden's intense growth.

Watering must be regular to get plants established, and should be long thorough soakings, not mere light sprinkles, so roots will grow deeply to follow the moisture. Once plants are established, a weekly soaking will suffice. In very dry hot weather the garden will need extra watering — two or three times a week, depending on the conditions — to maintain soil moisture. ❧

PHOTO: LEIGH CLAPP. PICTURED AT LAMBLEY NURSERY, VIC. AUSTRALIA

GARDEN SUMMARY

aspect full sun **climate** temperate or Mediterranean **soil** deep, rich, well mulched
water a good soaking every few days
photographed in autumn (main picture), early summer (small picture)
maintenance high

1 EASTER/MICHAELMAS DAISY

Aster x *frikartii* 'Mönch'
A summer- and autumn-flowering short-stemmed cultivar, the flowers are rich blue-mauve. Trim off spent flowers and lift to divide in early spring.

2 BERGAMOT

Monarda didyma 'Kardinal'
Purplish spires 50 to 100cm tall dress this perennial clump through summer into autumn. Keep trimming dead flowers and damaged stems. Divide and re-establish in early spring.

3 SALVIA

Salvia 'Indigo Spires'
This salvia will grow into a 1.5m space. It flowers generously with 30cm spikes of purplish blooms from spring to autumn, especially if spent flowers are trimmed off. Regular trimming of stems will keep it shapely. Take cuttings in autumn and prune in early spring.

4 RUSSIAN SAGE

Perovskia atriplicifolia 'Longin'
A light blue haze in summer tops this grey, fine-leafed clumping plant. The many stems can reach 1m. Trim back at the end of flowering and mulch well. Clumps can be divided in early spring.

5 EASTER/MICHAELMAS DAISY

Aster cordifolius 'Silver Spray'
This is the taller growing form of the first plant listed and will need a stake to keep stems upright. Trim and divide as previously described.

6 DAHLIA

Dahlia hybrids
There are many forms, heights and colours of dahlia. Seen here is a double-petalled tall red with upright flower heads, a lower growing single white with prominent yellow centre and on the other side with yellow blooms is 'Lime Glow'. For information on growing dahlias see page 9.

7 FLAX

Phormium 'Anna Red'
It will grow to 2m and has taller flowering stems in summer. They open a dull red but persist as woody features until pruned off. Leaf strips are useful as a tie when staking and to string up bulbs or flowers for drying.

8 GAURA

Gaura lindheimeri
This hardy perennial produces bushy heads of long-stemmed white-tinged pink flowers that nod in the breezes from spring until autumn. Trimming back original flower spikes induces new flowering offshoots. They are long-lasting in a vase. Cut back to the pink-blotched foliage at end of flowering and divide every couple of years.

9 SEDUM

Sedum 'Autumn Joy'
Growing throughout spring and summer, this plant becomes a clump of grey-green leafed stems about 30cm tall. Lime green buds open as masses of red-pink star clusters in autumn. Trim back to ground level after flowers fade and mulch well. They will need division every two years in early spring.

10 PRAIRIE SWITCH GRASS

Panicum virgatum 'Rubrum'
A soft haze of grass flowers which start as dusty pink and age to reddish seeds, top this green weeping grass. One specimen planted in early spring will fill a 40cm space. Trim right back to ground level the next spring and let it recommence. It can be divided but keep roots damp during the transplant.

11 JOE-PYE-WEED

Eupatorium maculatum 'Gateway'
Reddish-pink heads of blossom in autumn top the dark red 2m stems of this perennial. Trim back to ground level after flowering. The clump can be divided or moved in early spring, but if left undisturbed will become taller and more robust. A new plant can be seen at the front left.

12 BUTTERFLY BUSH

Buddleia davidii
This evergreen shrub has white-backed willowy leaves and terminal spikes of scented magenta blossom. A few flowers appear in spring, they mass in summer and follow through to autumn if the shrub is regularly trimmed. Bees and birds love it, as well as butterflies. Prune it back hard in early spring to prevent it becoming too straggly and to keep it confined to its designated space. Hard pruning will also result in more flowers. Cuttings taken in summer will provide new plants.

13 CONEFLOWER

Rudbeckia lanciniata
A wild yellow splash of colour is provided by this perennial with its purple-black cone centres. Allow 1m per plant. It will grow 1 to 2m tall.

14 AGAPANTHUS

Agapanthus 'Blue Giant'
Seen here are the finished flower heads maintained as accent features in the border. Growing from strappy leaf bases, the leafless flower stems stand tall, topped by conical buds. They open in summer and release a mass of blue trumpet-shaped flowers. Cut them for vases or leave as accents as seen here. Feed generously for lush development and plentiful flowers.

15 PENSTEMON

Penstemon hartwegii cultivars
The white flowering one is well decked, its red flowered neighbour just getting going. Plant in 50cm area in spring. Pinch out early growth for more stems and hence more flowers. The stems stand 30 to 50cm high and will be self supporting on a massed plant. Charming tubular flowers progress up the stem. Mulch well in cold areas. Trim back when dividing in early spring.

16 VERBENA

Verbena cultivars
A low-growing, purple-flowering perennial that spreads and suckers as it goes, it is probably best to start from new divisions each spring. Flat heads of buds on stem ends open throughout spring, summer and autumn. It's a useful "tuck in" plant.

17 CENTAUREA

Centaurea hypoleuca 'John Coutts'
A grey-backed leafy perennial with flower stems 40 to 50cm high which bears thistle-like flowers in deep pink. A single plant will clump to fill 30cm after planting in early spring.

18 VERONICA

Veronica 'Sunny Border Blue'
This cultivar flowers continually from early summer to autumn, the flower spikes getting longer as the blooms progress upwards. They form a mat 30 to 50cm across.

19 CUPID'S DART

Catananche caerulea 'Alba'
A tufted-leafed perennial, after the white flowers die, the papery bracts remain. Plant as intertwining accents in spring. Trim back in autumn.

20 WORMWOOD

Artemisia 'Powis Castle'
This finely cut low-growing artemisia gives round hillocks of grey. It grows to a height of 30cm but will spread wider so keep it trimmed to its position.

21 CATMINT

Nepeta x *faassenii*
The grey-green leaves here form a 50 to 90cm wide mat but emerging soft blue mauve flower heads stand 10 to 15cm above it. It blooms in spring and early summer and if cut back, will probably repeat in autumn. Trim to control its rooting wanderings and pot new plants from these divisions.

22 LAMBS EARS

Stachys byzantina
Long pointed well-furred grey leaves just have to be called lambs ears. The clumping perennial will burst into furry spires of soft mauve flowers in summer, but it's the foliage which is this plant's main attraction. Trim the flower stems to ground level when they have faded in late autumn, any leaves that have become ragged and leggy offshoots should go too. The cluster will need to be replanted every two or three years to keep it looking good.

Here we see the same border in early summer, as the parade commences. Pinkish tones predominate at present. The early growth reveals plants that become obscured as the season continues: red yarrow, Achillea *'Cherry Ripe'; two creamy* Achillea *x* taygetea; *purple-blue spikes of* Salvia nemorosa *'Ostfriesland'; pink-mauve spires on the right* Linaria *'Natalie'; little pink edging* Dianthus *'Doris'; and a rose grown for its year-round good looks* Rosa *'Lily Freeman'. Startling purple leaves at the back are Judas tree* Cercis canadensis *'Forest Pansy'. Comparing the two is a charming demonstration of the changing scene in the same border through the year.*

PHOTO: LEIGH CLAPP

PARTERRE GARDEN

Impact and formality are created by the use of parterre, in a small space, as here, or on a large scale if you have a team of gardeners to assist! The shape and plants are up to you. Ask at your nursery if unsure about what will suit your conditions. The exuberance of the growth in the tropics makes such designs too demanding.

The plantings here demand full sun and well drained soil. Each spring, feed with pelleted poultry manure or slow release fertiliser. The screening hedges are used here for framing and privacy but are not essential to protect the plants selected.

A parterre garden needs to be neat to be effective. Once the garden is established, neatness is achieved by constant vigilance. Ivy, box and cotton lavender will need regular maintenance trimming, see page 7. As soon as the plants poke growing tips out of line, trim them. If left until it becomes a heavy pruning job, unfortunate stick ends will remain visible. The sedums will need thinning as they clump and grow out of confinement lines. Be sure when designing and planting to leave access for maintenance routines like trimming, thinning and soil enrichment. ∽

GARDEN SUMMARY

aspect full sun **climate** temperate, subtropical or Mediterranean
soil free draining **water** not demanding **photographed in** spring
maintenance medium

---

1 STONECROP

Sedum acre
Tiny pale green leaves on spreading stems form this low mat succulent, often known as 'Gold Moss'. Plant cuttings or established plants at 15cm intervals. They will quickly spread and will need frequent trimming. Stonecrop is frost-hardy.

2 SEDUM

Sedum glauca
This green-leafed rosette form is a different colour and texture from the stonecrop, which gives the garden an essential contrast. Select a variety from your nursery that will survive your conditions; all succulents need sun but some are not frost-tolerant. Plant individual rosettes 10cm apart. They will quickly fill the area and will need thinning twice a year.

3 COTTON LAVENDER

Santolina chamaecyparissus
An evergreen/evergrey shrub constantly trimmed back provides grey contrasts. Plant small specimens 30cm apart and trim immediately and then every month in spring and summer, reducing as growth slows during autumn. Winter should give you a break but don't let it get away from you in early spring. Regular trimming will prevent the yellow flowers appearing.

4 IVY

Hedera helix
Trained to wind over a wire cone the ivy becomes a central pillar. Plant three around each cone and train all stems up. Once covered, keep trimmed after each growth spurt, usually in spring and summer. Cut off stems creeping along the ground.

5 BOX

Buxus sempervirens
Trimmed lines of box form the low hedges. Buy small but branching plants or grow from cuttings sufficient to plant at 15 to 20cm intervals. They are not demanding plants but are very slow growing. Regular trimming will eventually give neat borders (see page 7 for more information on pruning).

Oleander forms the screening hedge in the foreground. It has been clipped to square shapes as part of the parterre. The screen on the right is cup and saucer vine, *Cobea scandens*, displaying a wild exuberance to contrast with the neat clipped shapes. Hippeastrum and plantain lilies, *Hosta* sp, are at the back.

SMALL AND SUNNY

A tiny courtyard exposed to the sun all day can look pretty all year when well planned and planted as this one is. Limited plant variety and colour give the impression of space.

Well draining but rich soil is required, so add compost or well-rotted manure, and mulch with fine bark chips or leaf mulch in spring and autumn. Apply pelleted poultry manure or complete plant food directly to the soil under the mulch each spring. Most plants here do not need frequent watering except for the roses which like a good long soak. An individual drip watering system for them would be ideal. The rest will be happy with once weekly deep watering. ∾

GARDEN SUMMARY

aspect full sun   **climate** temperate, Mediterranean or subtropical
soil free draining, well fed and mulched   **water** not demanding except for roses
photographed in spring   **maintenance** medium

---

1 SEASIDE DAISIES
Erigeron karvinskianus
Pink and white tiny daisies flower almost all year. Spaced along the front, 20 to 30cm apart, they will soon fill the gaps and will need regular trimming to remove dead lower branches and to maintain a neat edge.

2 FRENCH LAVENDER
Lavandula dentata
Lavender bushes, here planted 30cm apart, produce grey aromatic leaves and blue flowers most of the year. Trim both flowers and stems regularly, to prevent woody branches showing.

3 STANDARD ROSES
Rosa 'Iceberg'
Standard roses are used to lift the blooms above the other foliage, but the less expensive natural form would work just as well.

4 IRIS
Iris germanica
Grey sword-shaped foliage with white or blue flowers in spring give a central dramatic focus. Alternatively, Algerian iris, *Iris unguicularis*, would flower blue as a winter feature.

PHOTO: LEIGH CLAPP. DESIGNED BY GARDEN IMPRESSIONS, NSW, AUSTRALIA

THE ROCK POOL

Fitted into the hillside, this pool has its own man-made creek cascading over the rocky slope, naturalised by Australian shrubs, palms and grasses with ground covers softening hard edges.

*I*t looks like a natural bushland pool, yet has the designed advantage of wide pool surrounds for access, maintenance and relaxation.

The scene can be enjoyed and supervised from the house and deck. Where fencing is mandatory, the shrubby surrounds quickly obscure the hard lines.

The planting suits subtropical, temperate or Mediterranean areas, with soil well drained, mulched but not too heavily fed. Remember to use fertiliser suitable for Australian plants as others can kill them.

These plants like full sun. If intending to develop some sun protection for swimmers, check final plant heights, foliage cover and debris drop before positioning close to the pool. Don't forget that too much shade will shorten the swimming season, but filtered sun provides some protection and coolness during summer. ❧

GARDEN SUMMARY

aspect sunny
climate Mediterranean, subtropical
or temperate   **soil** well drained
water to establish, then weekly to wash off
pool chemicals   **photographed in** spring
maintenance low

1 COAST ROSEMARY

Westringia fruticosa

A grey-green, short-leafed shrub with white-touched mauve flowers in spring and summer. It can be trimmed to control its bulk or height.

2 CABBAGE TREE PALM

Cordyline australis

Tropical looking with long draping leaves, cordylines can grow about 12m high. They produce white sprays of perfumed flowers among the leaves in late spring. If well watered they will remain lush looking. Trim off dead lower leaves to keep the palm tidy.

3 FAN PALM

Washingtonia filifera

The glossy fan foliage on this palm suits the site but take care, it can reach 12m! Try lower-growing palms with similar fanning leaves, such as *Luculia gracilis* or *Rhaphis excelsa*, so they will not overwhelm.

4 DATE PALM

Phoenix caneriensis

With strappy, glossy leaves this classic palm tree will eventually grow too big for its site. Its smaller relative, the miniature or pygmy date palm, *Phoenix roebellini,* would be a better bet.

5 PORT WINE MAGNOLIA

Michelia figo

Planted for its spring perfume and evergreen round shape, it will grow to 3m. It will take gentle pruning. Grevilleas or hakeas also would give roundness and team well with the rugged rocky landscape.

6 LEMON-SCENTED MYRTLE

Darwinia citriodora

It will grow into compact 1m blue-green mounds with reddish tints during autumn and winter. In spring and summer, stem ends bear orange-red bristly flowers. The foliage has a delicious lemon scent.

7 GERALDTON WAX

Chamelaucium uncinatum

A fine-leafed wiry shrub that will grow to nearly 2m and carries nodding clusters of pink or white waxy flowers through winter and spring. A good cut flower and the harvesting trims it.

8 SEASIDE DAISY

Erigeron karvinskianus

Thoroughly weaving its fine stems and bright white and pink flowers all about, seaside daisy will eventually need a controlling trim. It will recover or seed itself to display again.

9 GROUND MORNING GLORY

Convolvulus mauritanicus

This spreading ground cover decorates and softens. Round leaves on soft stems carry mauve flowers through summer when in good sunlight. It will need trimming where it comes into contact with the water as the foliage will burn.

TROPICAL
SPLENDOUR

There are thousands of abundantly growing tropical plants that give colour, perfume and lushness to tropical gardens. But even if you live in cooler conditions it's possible to successfully grow many tropical plants as long as you protect them from cold winds and frost. Plant them in pots and move them into the house, conservatory or glasshouse for the winter.

◀ BRIGHT COLOUR

Of the many common names given to this vine, tango poi seems the most exotic. Remember its proper name, *Pyrostegia venusta*, when buying it. This vigorous evergreen climber will quickly cover a fence or unsightly shed and gleam through winter and spring with golden-orange blooms. Plant in full sun in a frost-free location.

▼ MIXED COLOUR

A couple of magnificent elephant ears, green *Alocasia* x *amazonica* and pink *Caladium* x *hortulanum* are teamed with the purple-leafed *Tradescantia pallida* 'Purple Heart'. A philodendron weaves its heart-shaped leaves along the rail.

▲ FRAGRANT

Frangipani, richly leafed and always gloriously perfumed, is a tropical delight, seen here in its pink-flowered form. It grows as a tree to about 5m with a rounded head and will remain evergreen in the tropics. It's deciduous in cooler climes, but sadly will not tolerate frost. White, red and gold colourings are available.

▲ MIXED PLANTING

Most of the permanent colour in this garden is derived from the leaf colours of an assortment of variegated bromeliads. Odd seasonal changes are provided by showy flowers or coloured highlights in the central leaves (bracts) which attract pollinators to less gaudy blooms. The spreading arms are a *Dracaena draco* and the lower bright torch is a *Dracaena marginata* cultivar. All are best in tropical or sheltered subtropical gardens but it would be possible to grow them in cooler areas in a glasshouse.

TEMPERATE COTTAGE

*A sea of pinky mauves washes this garden corner in spring in lapping wave curves,
beside a grassy shore. The wallflower continues its winter spread,
when only bare twigs of berberis and rose, green background shrubs
and straps of red hot poker leaves were in evidence
Later, penstemon, Californian poppy and poker will feature before
autumn tints the scene. Anticipate changing colour waves.*

The soil is well mulched in winter with dressings of manure and autumn leaves. In late winter/early spring this is dug in to provide organic matter to aerate the soil and to hold moisture. Slow release pelleted poultry manure or complete plant food is added in spring and summer, carefully positioned on the soil under compost mulch. A long soaking watering is given once a week, more often if conditions are very hot and dry. All these plants need at least six hours of sun for best performance, and will survive both Mediterranean and subtropical conditions. ∽

GARDEN SUMMARY

aspect full sun **climate** temperate **soil** well mulched, rich, slow draining
water once weekly soaking **photographed in** late spring **maintenance** low

---

1 WALLFLOWER

Cheiranthus mutabalis
Growing into a shrub-like perennial, this plant has narrow grey-green leaves on masses of stems that usually need trimming to keep them tidy. During winter, spring and early summer it produces creamy pink scented flowers, ageing to deeper pink or cerise. A great bloomer, by early summer its flower stalks and leaf stems will be too long and will need a radical pruning back to almost ground level. Feed and water to encourage regrowth.

2 WATSONIA

Watsonia hybrids
These strappy-leafed plants grow from corms, a kind of bulb, and flower in late spring on spikes about 1.5m high. The leaves will brown off over summer and can then be removed; keep them until then to nourish the corm. Watsonia are native to South Africa and do not require extremes of cold or quantities of water to perform. However, they can become an invasive weed so don't use them in escaping gardens, see page 65, and dispose of excess corms wisely. They will need lifting and reducing every few years or will take up too much space. White and reddish forms are also available and the white form could be added to a scheme such as this.

3 PENSTEMON

Penstemon hartwegii hybrids
Green and bushy at the moment, and packed with potential, each stem will produce a succession of tubular flowers marching up the stem to the top. A single plant will become a clump if the tops are pinched out early as it starts to develop from winter dormancy. Colours are in the white, pink to red range.

4 WHITE MARGUERITE DAISY

Argyranthemum frutescens
Daisies have such a simple flower form, and so abundant a mass of them, they are an asset to any garden plan. To keep them producing longer, regularly pick them for vases and trim off finished flowering stems — the plant looks very unattractive wearing dead flowers, and deadheading will result in more flowers for a longer time. New plants are easy to strike from cuttings and can be used to replace old woody plants every two years. Marguerite daisies do not have a beautiful scent, but they are a sunny, happy addition to any garden and one of the easiest flowers of all to grow.

5 SEASIDE DAISY

Erigeron karvinskianus
A smaller daisy form on a lower growing clump, seaside daisy gives a white flower, ageing to pink. It can wander about among other plants or be trimmed into neat mounds. It flowers throughout the warm months.

6 GROUND MORNING GLORY

Convulvulus sabatius or *mauritanicus*
A cascading ground cover decked with mauve flat bells is seen here draping itself into the red hot poker, much like its cousin, morning glory, does. Its leaves are small and its stems are delicate so it does not suffocate other plants in the same manner, but it will need trimming at season's end. Mulch to protect it from severe frosts.

7 RED HOT POKER

Kniphofia uvaria
Another South African perennial, it is tolerant of coastal winds and cool to cold winters. The long strappy-leafed clump sends up tall flower spikes in summer with a poker-shaped head of red, orange or yellow tubular blooms. New cultivars provide a choice of colours. All must have full sun to bloom well. Trim off finished flower heads and ragged leaves annually and divide the clump to invigorate it every three or four years.

8 CALIFORNIAN POPPY

Eschscholzia californica
The hint of fine grey leaves seen behind the penstemon will produce open silky-petalled saucer-shaped flowers about 7cm across. Similar in appearance to the Iceland poppy, *Papaver nudicaule*, it is much easier to grow. Colouring can be yellow, cream, white or orange. Once you've got Californian poppies in your garden, you'll have them forever. This is an obliging self-seeding annual, flowering all summer and into autumn in its first year, and popping up to surprise you thereafter. It has a charming informality which perfectly suits the look of a cottage garden. Californian poppies can be picked for vases, but they don't last long.

PHOTO: GEOFFREY BURNIE. PICTURED AT MERLE HOWLETT'S GARDEN, GREENWELL POINT, NSW, AUSTRALIA.

9 ROSE

Rosa 'Albertine'
This meandering rose will climb trellises and trees using its many hooks on its many stems for assistance. Brownish-pink buds open to pink informal roses that fade as they age. They mass the plant in late spring but only remain for a few weeks. Perhaps a repeat flowering rose like a climbing 'Souvenir de la Malmaison' or 'Cymbeline' could produce a longer display.

AUTUMN TREES

Fabulous autumn colour like this is the final show of the growing year in temperate, cool or cold gardens. And such a show – is it magic or science? It appears magically but the scientists tell us it's to do with the bright sunny days and cold nights of autumn.

Sunny days allow plants to continue to produce food for growth. The cool nights produce a thickening on each leaf attachment point so the food is no longer transported through the plant. These trapped substances become the bright colours in the leaves.

Then the leaves fall, creating beautiful highlights, soft carpets and wonderful mounds to whoosh through and to compost. They can also be perceived as an enormous nuisance, but there are not many among us who don't appreciate the show.

For a garden like this to thrive, the climate should be cool, and the soil should be rich, light and warm, just as it would be in deciduous forests or woods where leaves have dropped and decomposed for many hundreds of years. All trees and shrubs planted for their autumn colouring should be in full sun or at least most of a day's sunshine, for best results. ❧

GARDEN SUMMARY

aspect full sun
climate temperate
soil rich, deep
water to establish
photographed in autumn
maintenance low

1 JAPANESE FLOWERING CHERRY

Prunus serrulata 'Shirotae'
The largest trunk is delightfully polished all year. The wide spreading canopy of leaves turns yellow, then golden-orange in autumn. In spring it presents clusters of single, white, fragrant blossoms. As in autumn the ground is carpeted, but at that time in white. The thinner dark trunk is a deep pink, double-blossomed variety, *Prunus serrulata* 'Fugenzo'.

2 WEEPING BIRCH

Betula pendula
The straight white trunk belongs to a weeping birch, growing straight and high in this woodland to compete for light. Not a "weep" in sight, but the elegance of its trunk is in nice contrast to the cherry's dark wood.

3 JAPANESE MAPLE

Acer palmatum
Bright spots of red and orange leaf colour come from a collection of assorted forms of Japanese maples, all varieties of which have spectacular autumn foliage. Their finely-cut, delicate leaves make a beautiful carpet.

4 VIOLETS

Viola odoratum
A charming deep-green ground cover, violets will wander among rocks, roots and shaded areas, clothing their clumps in heart-shaped leaves throughout the year, and heavily perfumed purple flowers in late winter and spring. They can get over-zealous in their ground covering role and will need digging out when gone too far.

5 AZALEAS

Azalea indica and *Azalea kurume*
Azaleas are among the few flowering plants that thrive under trees. And they're seen at their best in natural settings. Both these evergreen azaleas edge the pathways here and will join the cherries in a spring extravaganza of pink and white blossom.

Red Japanese maple leaves have gathered for the last of their autumn glory, dusting the rocks, garden, seat and pathway.

The other treasure of autumn in cool gardens are nerines. Seen here are Nerine bowdenii, *in deep pink and white. The bulb produces strappy leaves in spring that grow in the shade and its flower stems emerge in autumn, when sunlight starts to make its way in. The cluster of flowers have wavy edges, recurved tips to the petals and prominent stamens, making them curiously spiky. Pistachio, Chinese tallow and liquidambar can present warmer gardens with some autumn colour and* Zephyranthes candida, *with autumn-flowering crocus-like blooms, would provide an alternative to nerines.*

PHOTO: JAIME PLAZA

THE COLOUR PURPLE

Bright purple makes a striking impact in the garden, but has even more zing when teamed with a contrasting colour. Muted purples look wonderful when partnered by muted shades.

▼ PURPLE AND WHITE

White is a vital colour enhancer, contrasting, breaking up intensity and gleaming in the night light. Here two spring flowers combined draw attention to each other, the purple native iris, *Patersonia occidentalis*, and a white freesia, *Freesia refracta alba*.

◄ PURPLE AND RED

Vivid intensity of red rose campion, *Lychnis coronaria*, is teamed here with an equally vivid spiderwort, *Tradescantia* 'Purple Dome', for a rich summer show. It's hard to imagine the subtle contrast of grey campion leaves and green straps of this partner during winter.

▲ PURPLE AND LIME

The strong purple tones in this sage, *Salvia officinalis* 'Purpurascens', seen on its new foliage, contrast magnificently with the lime foliage of *Helichrysum petiolare* 'Aureum'. This strong lime colouring remains all year, and the arching stems will wander all among the sage.

PURPLE AND PINK ►

A less intense purple on the penstemon blends with the softly mauve pink of the poppy, *Papaver somniferum*. The sharp acid green of the spurge, *Euphorbia polychroma* adds the complementary contrast.

THE BOY AND THE BIRD BATH

Classical ornamentation has been used to set the stage for this simple but finely detailed planting and forms a cushion for the modest boy and his bird bath dish.

Colour choice is strictly adhered to, appearing most "whitened" in spring, as the lilies and azaleas join the endlessly flowering busy lizzies. The dark green of the vertical cypresses and both small and large round topiary boxes provide formality. Sun shines into this court in the mornings only, preventing hot afternoon scorching.

The soil is slow draining, given complete plant food or pelleted poultry manure every six months and covered with at least 10cm of fine bark chips each time.

This garden needs ample moisture which would be well provided by a trickle watering system. By this means, the plant roots will be well soaked but the flowers will not be water damaged. ∾

PHOTO: LEIGH CLAPP. DESIGNED BY GARDEN IMPRESSIONS, NSW, AUSTRALIA

GARDEN SUMMARY

aspect early sun, afternoon shade **climate** Mediterranean, temperate or subtropical
soil rich, damp **water** frequent **photographed in** spring **maintenance** medium

---

1 BUSY LIZZIE
Impatiens cultivar
Select a low-growing, large-flowered variety and plant at 12cm intervals. May die down in cold conditions.

2 AZALEA
Azalea indica 'Alba Magna'
A hardy azalea, with gently perfumed

flowers, it can grow large but is control-pruned after flowering to maintain its place here for a few years.

3 ARUM LILY
Zantedeschia aethiopica 'Crowborough'
Lush dark green leaves, all year in most conditions, only need an occasional tidying trim. A succession of gorgeous

white spathes stand bird-like above the leaves for a couple of months.

4 BOX TOPIARY
Buxus sempervirens
The small plants at the front are planted at 15cm intervals to maintain individual dome shapes. Two larger specimens at the back repeat the

shaping of the stone balls. See page 7 for information on shaping.

5 CYPRESS
Cupressus sempervirens
Densely green, pruned at the top to prevent tapering and "lean" problems, and regularly trimmed lightly all over, they frame the boy dramatically.

THE GRASS GARDEN

People used to keep grass only on the flattened mown area in their gardens, calling it "the lawn". The big battle was to keep it out of the garden. But now grass is "in", and in gardens at that.

*N*ot the old couch, kikuyu, buffalo or creeping bent, but attractive plants in their own right, planted individually or in sweeps. Plan to make use of varied leaf shapes, colours and forms. Their generous and lasting flower heads are another feature, as seen here, enduring right through winter. This picture was taken in autumn, in a subtropical garden. All the grasses used here will also do well in both temperate and Mediterranean climates.

There's very little maintenance needed: trim them down to almost ground level in early spring, mulch the trimmings around them with a feed of pelleted poultry manure underneath, and they will fountain back with fine green leaves to start, followed by lengthy stems and flowers. ～

GARDEN SUMMARY

aspect full to half a day's sun   **climate** temperate, subtropical and Mediterranean
soil moderately free draining   **water** to get grasses established
photographed in autumn   **maintenance** low

1 PANICUM
Panicum virgatum 'Rotstrahlbusch'
Glossy long leaves about 1cm wide sweep from the central clump. It will expand and can be divided. Long flower stems stand above the leaves in early summer to develop into reddish seed heads. To plant as a swathe like this, space 15 to 20cm apart. They will be dense enough to become a mass of leaves and to support the flower and seed heads draped over the top.

2 PENNISETUM
Pennisetum 'Hamelyn'
Fine leaves about 75cm long emerge from this clumping grass. During summer dusty pink flower plumes reach above the leaves, expanding and massing through to autumn — it makes a spectacular show when planted in a sweep. Pennisetum does best in full sun but will flower in some shade. Space at about 15cm for a sweep, or plant individually as accents beside rocks, tree trunks or reflecting pools.

PHOTO: LEIGH CLAPP. DESIGNED BY MICHAEL COOKE. NSW. AUSTRALIA

3 SEDUM

Sedum 'Autumn Joy'
Not a grass but a hardy succulent that has been used here as a foil to its neighbours; in spring with its greyish round leaves, summer with apple-green bud growth, and now with its undulating clouds of rosy pink flowers. Best planted as a group or sweep, it will enlarge the cluster with age, and will need dividing every few years.

PHOTO: LEIGH CLAPP

THE GARDEN IN SUMMER

The scene here is dominated by various greens. Sedum is developing buds, light and airy in apple green drifts. Miscanthus sinensis 'Gracillimus' is a dominant mound of shining green, awaiting its autumn cape of flower plumes that stand 2m tall.
Smaller and more upright is the variegated foliage of a group of Calamagrostis acutiflora 'Overdam', with a reddish Carex petrii behind them. All are useful accent plants or groupies. The purple-leafed form is an annual Perilla frutescens 'Atropurpurea', planted each year as a contrast.

A SHADY CORNER

Abundant moisture, rich fertile soil and shady protection make this lush garden possible. This is a temperate garden but something similar can be created in most climate zones as long as the three conditions are met.

Frequent water must keep the air and roots damp. The leaves of these plants will burn and shrivel if the air is hot and dry. Soil must have a deep layer of decomposing leaf and bark mulch to maintain cool moist roots. Add more as plants expand. Apply liquid indoor plant food like fish emulsion during spring and summer to keep leaves growing lushly. Shade and protection are provided by surrounding shrubs and a rocky outcrop. Screening lattice can be used for wind and sun protection. Make sure protective shrubs will filter the sun. A deciduous tree would offer the perfect summer protection, supply leaf mulch in autumn, and allow winter light through. ◡

GARDEN SUMMARY

aspect sheltered **climate** temperate **soil** moist **water** essential
photographed in spring **maintenance** low

---

1 RHODODENDRON
Rhododendron cultivar
A shrub with dense dark green foliage which likes shady, moist environments. A tree above would screen harsh sunlight. Rhododendrons produce showy spring flowers.

2 HYPERICUM
Hypericum patulum 'Hidcote'
This wandering arm of hypericum will produce open yellow flowers among the leaves. Its height, less than a metre, protects the ferns.

3 PLANTAIN LILY
Hosta undulata, var. *univittata*
Several plants here form a generous display. Plantain lily dies down in winter and re-emerges each spring. Be watchful as slugs and snails attack the early leaves. Philodendrons would suit tropical areas.

4 FERNS
Two ferns, *Asplenium scolopendrium* and *Athyrium filix-femina* have been used here. When selecting yours from your nursery, choose a couple of contrasting forms to give a good display with varied foliage.

COASTAL GARDEN

This delightful grey garden is planted on a slope facing a full day's sun. The background of deep blue is the sea across which can whip wild winds, cold in winter and very drying in summer. The plants used here can cope with such conditions and maintain their dramatic and artistic arrangement.

Soil on a slope must be well secured, either with layered beds that become obscured as vegetation grows, or by positioning mulch-mat fibre or netting with the initial planting to keep soil in place until roots bind it. Three centimetres of coarse mulch over the surface will also keep soil from blowing or flowing away in wind or downpours. As well it will maintain moisture and break down slowly to add organic matter to sandy soil.

The plants used will need regular water to get them established and should then be able to survive without watering, except for occasional soakings in long dry spells. Grey-leafed plants feature because they can cope with sun and dry conditions. Blue, white and yellow colourings predominate, with the odd touch of purple in flowers and leaves, adding highlights amid the varied greys. ❧

GARDEN SUMMARY

aspect full sun   **climate** temperate,
Mediterranean or subtropical
soil free draining, well mulched
water to get plants established
photographed in summer
maintenance medium

thistle looks dramatic. The purple flowers should be cut before they dry and distribute their seed, a habit which has caused their reputation as a weed.

6 CARDOON
Cynara cardunculus
More spiky points on each leaf than on the thistle but a similar silvery coat gives this plant contrast yet compatibility. Give it a metre to fill and trim back after flowering, wearing long protective sleeves and gloves. Dispose of the foliage of both this and the thistle deep in compost piles to avoid unexpected spikes.

7 ECHIUM
Echium pininana
Long tapering spires with leaflets arranged among the buds reaching up to 4m high are a stunning focus in this garden. The blue flowers open slowly up the stems during summer. The spires can remain untrimmed until the next flower heads start to emerge. One plant can spread its reaching branches over nearly 3m.

8 YELLOW LUPINS
Lupinus arboreus
These lupins are on a shrub that grows in a sprawling manner to about 1.5m. Foliage is soft and divided but will become untidy during winter. However, in spring it thickens up and sweetly-scented flowers appear in summer. Trim off seeds and one-third of its summer growth in autumn. It's best planted at the back of a bed.

9 DUSTY MILLER
Senecio viravira
Well dusted stems and foliage make this a remarkably white plant. It will spread and mound to about 1m and has yellowish tufted flowers in summer.

10 CAMELLIA
Camellia sasanqua
Palest pink single blooms don't look out of place in this grey garden as the yellow flowers finish and the blues become dominant. Sasanquas are a fast growing early flowering camellia.

1 CURRY PLANT
Helichrysum italicum
This large spreading fine-leafed perennial smells of curry when brushed past. In summer it is topped with heads of yellow tufted flowers. Plant a group of curry plants in a foreground position, (they grow about 1m high) at 30cm intervals. Trim off by a third before flowers become tatty. They can be used in dry arrangements.

2 DELPHINIUMS
Delphinium elatum
Soft divided foliage is a great contrast to the greys. These perennials will need extra moisture to keep them lush and will reward with spires of blue flowers in summer standing up to 2m tall. Cut for vases or trim back low and mulch and manure richly for follow-on flowerings.

3 BRONZE FENNEL
Foeniculum vulgare 'Purpureum'
Soft feathery foliage coloured reddish-purple grows from bulbous clumping stems and is topped in late summer with flat yellow flower heads. A single plant will develop into a clump up to 1m round.

4 PLECTRANTHUS
Plectranthus argentatus
Velvet grey leaves cover the stems over this lax low perennial. In autumn it sends up fine spires of mauve and white flowers. One plant can cover a metre in a season. Trim back stems that wander too far.

5 SCOTCH THISTLE
Onopordium acanthium
Strongly growing up to flower, and dressed in its spiky silvery leaves the

SCENTED LEAVES

Leaves to brush past, leaves to crush, leaves to dry for potpourri and leaves to use in cooking,
there are hundreds of scented leaves that can serve their purpose in your garden.
They are often subtle additions but some are interestingly coloured, shaped
or flowered and any are worth including in your scheme.

◀ LAVENDER

Lovely lavender perfume can be enjoyed all year when plants are positioned near walkways as the leaves are often as pungent as the blooms. Allards lavender, *Lavandula allardii*, is the strongest, but French, *L.dentata*, and English, *L.angustifolia*, are good too. Prune them back after flowering to keep the shape neat.

ERIOSTEMON ▶

This small Australian shrub is usually planted for its mop of white-tinged pink flowers in winter/spring and its ability to thrive in most conditions. But please plant your *Eriostemon myoporoides* near a pathway so it can be brushed in passing to enjoy its year-round waxy sweet aroma.

◀ LEMON BALM

Lemon balm, *Melissa officinalis*, in its neat early growth makes a rounded cushion of lemon-scented leaves. Use fresh for a lemony addition to stuffings or salads and dried for potpourri or tea. The tea, taken daily, is said to soothe the nerves and promote longevity. As it gets older the clump extends and flowers, attracting bees to the garden.

PELARGONIUMS ▶

Scented geranium leaves, (actually pelargoniums) come in many shapes, colours and perfumes. Large and crinkled could be lime, lemon, cinnamon, apricot or rose; felty and flat will be peppermint; tiny could be apple, ginger, lemon, coconut or nutmeg. There's also herby scents like woodruff and southernwood, the list goes on. These leaves are all delightful in a mixed bunch.

RUSSET TONES

A section of a perennial border showing a cluster of autumn plants, taking over from but intermingling with the last notes of the summer performers. There is always something of interest happening in this garden.

The plants shown here will thrive in full sun, in temperate as here, subtropical and Mediterranean conditions. None is particularly choosy about soil apart from needing good drainage. But obviously a perennial border supporting a succession of major plants in good condition throughout a year will need regular feeding. These plants will tolerate an occasional dry spell once they are established. Apply complete plant food or slow release poultry pellets in spring and late summer. Spread mulch to cover.

GARDEN SUMMARY

aspect full sun, screened from drying winds **climate** temperate, Mediterranean, or subtropical **soil** well drained and well nourished **water** sufficient for spring establishment, but not so much to develop massive leaf display. Let the soil dry out once plants are growing **photographed in** autumn **maintenance** medium

---

1 SNEEZEWEED

Helenium 'Moerheim Beauty'
These strikingly coloured flowers start to open in late summer and autumn. In full sun one plant spreads generously to 1m or more; the bigger the clump, the denser the flowers. Divide in late winter or early spring.

2 STIPA

Stipa gigantea
A graceful specimen grass which develops leaves 30cm long. It remains brightly green all year but the flower spikes standing tall in summer develop straw coloured graceful airy heads that look attractive right through winter. Trim back hard in early spring.

3 CROCOSMIA

Crocosmia 'Lucifer'
Growing from a corm, these strappy leaves shoot in spring and produce long flower stems with arching branched spikes of red bell-like flowers and buds over summer. The seeds that then develop remain a feature and both the fresh flowers and seed heads look good in vases. Let the leaves remain until shrivelled to nourish the corm. Lift when dormant if needing to reposition or reduce the clump.

4 PURPLE ORACH

Atriplex hortensis 'Rubra'
Reddish-purple leaves, stems and flowers clothe this free-seeding annual. It can flower and seed two or three times a year, so once you've planted seed in spring you're away. It will shine in a russet-toned border with seed heads reaching 1.5m. Pull them out when too ragged.

5 DAHLIA

Dahlia 'Bishop of Llandoff'
Another touch of purple leaves in this dahlia cultivar which flowers bright red. See page 9 for growing details.

6 JOE-PYE-WEED

Eupatorium maculatum 'Gateway'
A beautiful dusty pink cloud of this shrubby Joe-pye-weed is at the back. It starts to flower in summer and will form a dense clump if left undisturbed for a few years. But do prune it back at the end of autumn.

7 NASTURTIUM

Tropaeolum majus
Grown here for its leaf shape and wandering habit, it adds contrast and can hide plants folding up for winter before tidying pruning begins. In this scheme, any nasturtium colour will suit. They will self seed and may need some serious culling.

8 MONKSHOOD

Aconitum cultivar
This grows as a clumping perennial, happy in some shade. Tall spires of purple-hooded flowers appear in summer and autumn. All parts of monkshood are poisonous.

THE SERIOUS VEGETABLE GARDEN

Serious, well maintained, productive and attractive, what more could one ask of a vegetable garden. Note that we've used the word, garden, not merely a patch. It has design details like trimmed mophead camellias, tripods of sweet peas and clipped box hedges leading to the cutting garden beyond. One small complaint — there are no paths from which to gather such bounty!

*T*his temperate climate garden was pictured in early summer. Trees and walled surrounds have provided protection and hurried on the development of tender plants, boosted by day-long sun.

Soil for vegetables is usually well dug and manured. Crops with differing demands on nutrients are then rotated through the beds so leaf crops will be replaced by fruit bearers then root crops. Leafy vegetables need weekly splashings of liquid manure to speed them to lushness. Water must be sufficient to keep all plants from wilting and is best applied early morning or late evening.

GARDEN SUMMARY

aspect full sun **climate** temperate **soil** well manured and dug **water** plentiful
photographed in early summer **maintenance** high

1 RUBY CHARD
Beta vulgaris
This is the red stemmed relative of silver beet. Seed or seedlings can be positioned as here, in rows 15 to 30cm apart after frosts. Water and feed regularly. In subtropical gardens they will grow all year.

2 ONIONS
Allium cepa
Onions do not require the same richly manured space as chard, but do like good drainage. Solve both needs by making a raised bank of unmanured loam then add slow release fertiliser. Plant seeds in autumn, thin them in spring, using the small green onions in cooking. Bulbs form in summer, harvest as you need them, and dry well when storing them. Beet or chard and onions are companion plants.

3 CARROTS
Daucus carota
Seen here in regimental rows with feathery plumed tops. Seed is planted directly in well dug and previously manured soil, as soon as it begins to warm in frosty zones. In other areas, plant year round. It is often sown with radish seed, these breaking through first to allow in air and water and provide a cover to reduce weed growth. When harvested there will be plenty of room for the carrots. Start thinning and harvesting early.

4 ROSEMARY
Rosmarinus officinalis
These well trimmed ornamental mounds contrast well with the carrots. Trimmings, of course are used in cooking. They have been placed about 1m apart.

5 SWEET PEAS
Lathyrus odoratus
Delightful and sweetly-scented, each sweet pea plant can produce up to 50 blooms. Planted here at each corner of the bamboo tripods, they will twine and become flowering pillars during summer. In warmer districts use nasturtium or purple beans.

A healthy swathe of potatoes grows beyond the rosemary, with frames behind for climbing plants like peas, beans or cucumbers. Peas and beans absorb nitrogen and store it in nodules on their roots. Dig the roots into the soil after harvest.

PHOTO: LEIGH CLAPP. PICTURED AT LAMBLEY NURSERY, VIC. AUSTRALIA

OLD-FASHIONED COTTAGE GARDEN

Cottage gardens certainly have charm with their meandering pathways, dense plantings, old fashioned varieties, colour masses and apparently unstructured design. Wandering through would reveal assorted scents and hidden treasures. It looks abundant, generous and casual. But don't be deceived. Careful colour choices, a knowledge of individual plant requirements, ultimate heights and flowering times are necessary for a successful display.

Ornaments, like the wrought iron bird bath seen here, add a focus. A sundial, seat or simply an open paved area would serve as well to break up the intensity of the planting. This garden is pictured in summer in a temperate climate zone, protected from fierce winds by the generous roof of the cottage and by the maple on the west. Sun washes over the garden during the day. Most of the plantings would adapt to Mediterranean or subtropical conditions.

The soil is well mulched with manure while plants are dormant in winter, and topped with a liberal dressing of leaves from the maple, which gives the garden an "I'm resting" look. The manure and decomposed leaves are dug in each spring with the new plantings of divided perennials and dahlias. Complete fertiliser added with each planting, and again in summer and autumn, will keep up the demands of the prolific growth seen here.

Watering is essential to get new growth under way, a good soaking twice a week as a minimum. Mulch with composted fine pine bark to reduce moisture loss. Later as plants grow higher, and roots longer, a weekly watering should suffice, but make it a long soaking, not a sprinkle.

Although the garden looks casual, it requires a lot of maintenance to keep up this cottagy overgrown appearance. There must be careful and regular trimming and tidying of new growth, checking for insect, slug and snail feasting and pinching back top heavy growth. But in such lovely surroundings, it's pleasurable work. Deadheading is another essential job, to keep the plantings attractive and to encourage new flower development to maintain the display. ✎

GARDEN SUMMARY

aspect full sun **climate** temperate **soil** rich, slow draining
water needs regular watering **photographed in** summer **maintenance** high

---

1 DAHLIA
Dahlia cultivar
The cultivar used here has handsome lush foliage and mass planted as here, awash with deep crimson flowers, it makes a striking impact. For information about planting see page 9. Tall-growing varieties like this need staking or the canes will bend, break or flop onto their neighbours. Trim off dead flowers or pick new blooms for vases. Always recut the stem just before placing in water to remove the air lock. Lift dahlia tubers if frost is a possibility, otherwise mulch heavily after stems are pruned in late autumn. In humid areas mildew on leaves can be a problem. Cannas might be a suitable alternative.

2 FEATHER REED GRASS
Calamagrostis 'Karl Foerster'
The upright form of this grass is even more pronounced when it flowers. The heads can reach 1.5m. Marvellous in summer, it is superb in winter, with the skeletons of the flowers holding on. It will survive frost and looks splendid iced up. Trim back to ground level in spring and a neat new clump will sprout, or simply trim off flowers and allow new growth to grow through the old. It is adaptable to most conditions. Plant as individual accent points.

3 PANICUM
Panicum virgatum 'Rotstrahlbusch'
This smaller grass has weeping lustrous green leaves and in summer produces red flowers and seed in open sprays. It will stand 50 to 80cm high and will clump out to a similar size. It is not demanding and copes with most climates but will appreciate extra water to get it established. Cut it back in spring or merely trim off flowers.

4 MISCANTHUS
Miscanthus sinensis 'Sarabande'
Tall and almost bamboo-like, these clump to about 1.5m and stand 2m tall in flower, seen here with pinkish colouring. This form has plain green leaves. Other forms have cream stripes down or across the leaves, giving a shadowy effect. They need water to get them established but will cope with most climates.

5 CONEFLOWER
Echinacea purpurea
This perennial likes rich moist soil and full sun to perform well. A cluster of plants, say five per square metre, planted in spring will produce a good display in summer. Their rich purplish-pink tones with the dahlia and grass head colours, and the simple daisy form with its cone-like centre is a nice contrast. They will spread out in clumps by the end of summer and will need dividing every four or five years. In drier conditions try sedum or valerian. For humid sites try purple alternanthera.

THE SALVIAS
The salvias used here are generous performers, flowering from late spring through to autumn. They enjoy a sunny position, reasonable soil and are not dependent on large supplies of water.

6 SALVIA
Salvia involucrata 'Bethellii'
This salvia has heads of magenta flowers. One plant given a square metre in spring will fill it by summer's end. It will need regular tidying trims, both to keep it shapely and encourage new blooms. Cut back heavily and mulch to protect it over winter. Rock rose might suit drier conditions and try ixora in humid zones.

7 MEXICAN SAGE
Salvia leucantha
This form has whitish furry stems and long felted grey leaves. Each stem is topped by purple velvet flower spikes. Plant the first clump in a metre space. The clump will spread and may need dividing at the end of flowering. Trim finished flower heads back to ground level. It will re-emerge after frosts.

8 BRONZE FENNEL
Foeniculum vulgare 'Purpureum'
This soft foaming purplish feature is a marvellous accent plant, particularly in this red/purple colour scheme. Sow seed and transplant, or use ready grown plants, placing three or four per square metre. They will develop in full sun to become a large clump. The foliage smells of aniseed. Flower spikes will emerge in summer standing up to 2m tall. They open as a flat candelabra with limey-yellow flowers, useful in vases. After flowering, trim down to ground level to tidy.

9 BUTTERFLY BUSH
Buddleia davidii cultivar
This rich pink form swells the pinkish highlights in the garden, growing as a shrub to 3 or 4m. It is positioned at the edge of this planting. Not very demanding as regards soil or water, it only needs full sun and regular trimming to keep it shapely and dressed with flowers. Butterflies and honeyeaters love it.

10 EASTER/MICHAELMAS DAISY
Aster lateriflorus var. *horizontalis*
A dense clumping perennial, usually flowering in autumn, hence its name change either side of the equator, it has been bred to produce flowers in summer in a stunning variety of colours and forms. Choose the right height, colour and flowering time to suit your plan and plant three per metre for a line of them or five per square metre for a cluster. Beware, some forms can become invasive so lift them in spring, remove all root stock from the soil and replant single rooted shoots each year. They make an excellent cut flower and picking will force new flowering. *Osteospermum* or *Arctotis* in the right colours might be easier to control.

11 PINCUSHION FLOWER
Scabiosa 'Pink Lace'
Greyish low foliage on this perennial produces emergent stems of buds which open to a pincushion tuft. Pink is used here, but mauve, purple and white forms exist. They appreciate a touch of lime in the soil. Plant every 30cm at the front of the display. Trim back after flowering. For humid areas try *Tradescantia pallida* 'Purple Heart'.

12 YARROW

Achillea millefolium 'Rosea'
If the Australian Snowy Mountains are anything to go by, this perennial likes open, sunny, dry conditions and isn't stopped by frost. It has become a major weed there on gravelly roadsides. But in your garden you stand a chance to control its wandering ways, grow lusher plants and be rewarded with flowering spikes of massed tiny daisies emerging from feathery grey/green foliage. There are many colour forms. Plant in spring 20 to 30cm apart. Flowering starts late spring, continuing until autumn. They last very well in vases. Break up the clumps, trim flower heads and runners and reposition new clumps in early winter or spring. Coleus or plectranthus varieties would be good substitutes in humid zones.

13 PENSTEMON

Penstemon cultivars
The green leafy stems on this perennial take it in turns to produce buds on the top third of their growth. These open progressively into tubular bells. They have a willowy gentle charm. Plant as specimens or in clusters 20cm apart in spring, in rich, moist soil in good sun. Pinch out the top of early stems to thicken the plant. Divide the clump every two years at least. Gaura will cope with drier conditions, and try red bromeliads in humidity.

14 TOBACCO FLOWER

Nicotiana hybrids
An annual, planted out each spring, this cluster of about five plants per square metre has produced an accent point of lime green. There are many varieties available so choose colour and height to suit. The yellow is a pleasing contrast and will be joined by more yellow flowers in autumn. They need good sun, ample moisture and rich soil. Flowers have a delicate perfume. Shrubby golden-leafed cherry pie would be a permanent rather than annual substitute, and a limey-leafed coleus could stand in for humid zones.

15 CATMINT

Nepeta 'Six Hills Giant'
This perennial loves full sun on a path or garden edge and will dress about 60cm with soft grey foliage. This form has flower heads that reach that same height. Trim back after flowering. Humid zones could try eau de cologne mint contained, to prevent escape, in a buried pot.

FAST GROWING PLANTS

Selected here are a very few fast growing plants that are useful in filling gaps, making an impact or adding that extra colour or shape in a very quick time.

◀ **SUNFLOWERS**

Giants of stem, leaf and flower, a fabulous display like this comes in summer from spring seed planting. These are *Helianthus annuus* with a single flower. Mexican sunflowers, *Helianthus* x *multiflorus*, are similar but have many flowers on each stem. All sunflowers like sunny conditions and will be far more robust if planted in rich soil and given some additional water.

COLEUS AND BUSY LIZZIES ▶

A lovely combination to quickly fill a shaded or partly shaded corner. They can become a permanent display in a tropical climate or a summer addition to a cooler temperate garden and can move to bright indoors or sheltered positions as the weather cools. Both will easily strike from cuttings taken in late summer or autumn.

▲ LIMEY SPURGE

This superb perennial, *Euphorbia characias wulfenii*, grows almost shrublike with stems about 1m long, each topped by a generous head of yellow and limey flowers. Prune back hard after its spring flowering. It's a wonderful accent plant teamed with blue, grey, mauve or white. There are annual forms as well.

▲ LOLLIPOP PLANT

The yellow bracted spikes stand up straight and the white flowers push through the spikes on this shrubby tropical *Pachystachys lutea*. It grows well in semi-shade, given good water and a damp position. In drier conditions the yellow shrimp plant, *Beloperone guttata lutea*, is a good substitute. Both make an impact quickly and flowers last well.

GREVILLEA ▶

Seen sometimes as trees — the mighty silky oak, *Grevillea robusta* — but more usually as shrubs as here, *Grevillea* 'Superb', grevilleas quickly and showily grow to fill a space or create a screen. They flower almost non-stop and varieties are available for most climate zones. They thrive in full sun in well drained soil. Their nectar-rich blossoms attract birds.

GUM TREE GARDEN

Peace and tranquillity prevail in this soothing garden scene. One can smell the leaves underfoot and hear the swish of those above, along with the buzz of a cicada or two.

This juvenile stand of Eucalypts, planted only three years previously from tube stock, is planned to become a serpentine avenue of smooth white trunks with a billowing foliage crown. Understorey plantings are the hangers-on from what was once full sun, fast becoming shade, as the trees mature. It is anticipated that eventually gravel and leaf litter will be the ground cover, forming a natural ambience and certainly less maintenance. The plantings seen here will thrive in Mediterranean, temperate and subtropical conditions, but do best in light to medium, well drained soils. It is wise to plant to suit your own soil type and weather peculiarities if these conditions do not apply. Eucalypts have developed to suit every situation so there will be plenty to choose from. You can select leaf, flower or fruiting features as well as trunk details for your garden. Understorey plantings could of course be Australian native plants also, forming a bush scene, or a mix of native and exotic. ❧

GARDEN SUMMARY

aspect full sun   **climate** temperate, Mediterranean or subtropical   **soil** free draining
water to establish only   **photographed in** spring   **maintenance** low

---

1 GUM TREES
Eucalyptus scoparia
Elegant white trunks growing to about 15m are topped by a willowy open

crown. Inconspicuous whitish flowers open in summer.

2 MONDO GRASS
Ophiopogon japonicus
A low growing draping grass that spreads by underground stems. It can be maintained as an edging by removing offshoots or can be allowed to interweave with other plantings. It is happy in semi-shade or sun.

3 WATSONIA
Watsonia hybrids
Strappy leaves emerge from a corm each spring to develop spikes with many tubular flowers progressing up the stem in late spring or early summer. The colour here is white, but pinks, orange and yellow forms exist.

PHOTO: LEIGH CLAPP. DESIGNED BY MICHAEL COOKE. NSW. AUSTRALIA. PICTURED AT HAWTHORN STUD

4 ALOE
Aloe arborescens
This prickly mound of blue-green "octopi" will continue to clamber over itself as long as there is sufficient sun. Each rosette sends out spikes of red flowers in late winter, a nice flame in the chill.

5 LOVE-LIES-BLEEDING
Amaranthus caudatus
Long tassels of wine-red tiny flowers hang from this bushy annual during summer and autumn. Plant seed or seedlings in spring in light but manured soil. Position them as accents in good sunlight, allowing room for 50cm spread and 1m height. Pull them out when plants become untidy.

6 GERMANDER
Teucrium fruticans
Surprisingly, the germander is still doing well in the partial shade. Planted as a casual hedge either side of the steps, its fine grey foliage and wonderful angular spread continues the subtle colour plays in this scene.

PHOTO: LEIGH CLAPP

This Eucalypt is a scribbly gum, Eucalyptus haemastoma, *with "writing" on the smooth bark. Japanese anemones,* Anemone x hybrida *shelter in the semi shade provided and give autumn highlights and their companion, white ginger lily,* Hedychium coronarium, *scents the air in the summer months.*

FORMALITY AND FUN

A collection of madly painted bird boxes, set in a mass of varied foliage, decorates this gravel walk. A leafy embankment copes with the level change on the right. It's a nice mix of formality and fun. The cat's on his way to the catnip, knowing the birds are safely out of reach.

This temperate garden is pictured in summer with the growth densely greened. Imagine it in autumn, or in winter's stark bareness, perhaps snow-dappled. Spring would show a wash of blossom.

There are different soil conditions here. The slope on the right drains fast. Moisture gathers on the left in a hollow, accommodating the plantings used there. A mulch of leaves and manure is added before each winter to break down for spring regrowth.

Complete or slow release fertiliser is added around existing plantings as they start to re-emerge. It should also be used with any replacement or new plantings that are added throughout the growing year.

GARDEN SUMMARY

aspect full sun, shade from trees   **climate** temperate to cool temperate

soil well mulched, damp patch suitably planted

water protect during dry spells   **photographed in** summer

maintenance medium

---

1 PEAR
Pyrus species
A fruiting or ornamental pear can be used in this position. Select one to suit your needs and conditions. All produce rich white clusters of blossom in spring and autumn leaf colour.

2 WISTERIA
Wisteria chinensis or *W. floribunda*
Choose from white, pink or blue varieties which will densely cascade in spring from bare twisting boughs. In summer trim off outrageous reaching stems or twine them into the existing vine. It will become a weighty vine, so make sure its support is strong.

3 ORNAMENTAL ONION
Allium varieties
Strappy leaves from bulbs produce pink, mauve or red flower spikes in summer which open as a mass of stars in a big ball. The leaves die down in winter and will re-shoot in spring. As flowers fade seeds develop on the "ball" as seen here. They look striking left on the plant and can also be cut for stunning winter dry arrangements. Some allium flowers smell like onions, but most don't. They are an unusual addition to the garden and look equally at home in an untidy effusive cottage setting or in a spare uncluttered design. Trim off at the end of autumn.

4 DAYLILIES

Hemerocallis cultivars
More strappy leaves, this time with brightly coloured trumpet flowers that open day by day for about 2 weeks' show, until another stem emerges. Plant in sun and mulch well for a moist root run.

5 IRIS

A beardless Pacific Coast hybrid like 'Purple Dream' or a Japanese iris like *delavayi*, will flower over summer and suit these conditions.

6 GARDEN PINK

Dianthus plumarius
The original species pink has exuberant green foliage with generously flowering stems. The sweetly scented flowers make exceptional cut flowers and last well in a vase. Delicate and floppy in growth pattern, the clump will spread generously so trim to tidy during summer and prune to almost ground level in autumn.

7 LAMBS EARS

Stachys byzantina
Furry grey leaves give a splash of brightness in a green border. Tall mauve flower spikes appear in summer, as seen here. Cut them back after flowering and trim the leaves to control the spread and to neaten.

8 BOX HEDGE

Buxus sempervirens
These evergreens are planted at 20 to 30cm intervals forming individual round guards. They are slow growing and require a light trimming twice a year to maintain their shape (see page 7 for more information on pruning).

9 SEDUM

Sedum spurium coccineum
The flash of red is a succulent. Select one to suit your conditions from your nursery, or take cuttings from a friend's garden. Some sedums are not frost-tolerant. They can be replaced if necessary each year.

10 BLUE WILD RYE

Elymus glaucus
The fine grey leaves contrast with the broader lambs ears opposite. *Elymus* is tolerant of dry conditions and frost and will form a round clump of about 1m.

11 GREATER STITWORT

Stellaria holostea
Stars of white dot this low spreading clump growing on the edge of the damp area. The stems will develop roots as they spread and may need controlling.

12 HEUCHERA

Heuchera americana 'Purple Palace'
This generous leafy clump with bronze-tinted foliage will spread to 30cm in rich moist soil. Fine spikes of white flowers appear in summer, but it's the leaves that provide the drama.

13 CAMPANULA

Campanula portenschlagiana
Violet bell-shaped flowers in spring and summer dress this attractive ground cover. It likes shade and damp and looks especially attractive spilling over the edge of the garden, as here.

14 PLANTAIN LILY

Hosta fortunei 'Aurea Marginata'
Variegated hostas bring light to a shaded area. They flourish and flower in shade in rich, moist soil and die down over winter, when they can be safely divided. Plantain lilies need slug and snail protection as leaves grow.

15 SUMMER FLOWERING LILIES

Spikes of buds rising in the shade will open their trumpets soon. They grow from a large scaled bulb which is best left undisturbed for a few years. Older bigger bulbs produce bigger flowers, and the effect is better when they have developed into a clump. Pick flowers for vases and mulch well with leaf litter as the plant dies down.

Creeping thyme clothes the steps, providing a softening effect and scenting the air with a pleasant aroma when crushed. As a bonus, it can be picked for cooking.

PHOTO: GEOFFREY BURNIE. PICTURED AT 'ARDEN WOOD'. VIC. AUSTRALIA

AUTUMN HYDRANGEAS

Most of us are familiar with hydrangeas in their first flush of colour in late spring or early summer; the shrub is often totally covered with great mopheads of flowers coloured pink, red, blue, mauve or white.

The intensity of the colour depends on the variety planted but the original colour may change as the roots settle into the acidity (inducing pink colouring) or alkalinity (blue colours) of your soil. White flowering plants remain unchanged. These early blooms may be cut to encourage a second flowering in late summer. If they're left on the plant they will age into beautiful muted colours in autumn. ∾

CONDITIONS FOR GROWTH
1 Deep rich soil, generously manured or compost-mulched during winter.
2 Shade, particularly from midday and afternoon sun, to prevent scorching.
3 Ample water. If soil is free draining keep digging in mulch. A thorough soaking around the roots is essential during dry spells in summer.
4 Pruning in late autumn or early winter in subtropical climates or early spring in temperate zones. Canes that have flowered should be cut back to the lowest pair of plump buds. Those that haven't flowered are left untrimmed unless they spoil the shape of the plant.

HYDRANGEAS
Hydrangea macrophylla
A long flowering shade-loving shrub that will be a feature as an individual specimen or massed planting for six to nine months of the year. There are many forms and cultivars available; select what appeals to you. They are easily propagated by planting stems in autumn. There are treatments sold by your nursery to change the pH of the soil thus changing the colour of the blooms. Their winter pruned bareness can be masked with underplantings of violets, hellebores, crinums or early spring bulbs.
Supporting the hydrangeas in their autumn flush here are cotoneaster berries fanned up the wall.

GARDEN SUMMARY
aspect east facing, shady **climate** subtropical or temperate **soil** deep, rich, moist
watering long soaking in dry spells **photographed in** autumn
maintenance medium

THE GREEN GARDEN

Away gaudy hues. The brilliance of this tropical garden is that while it's dressed only in a swathe of green, it's given variety and texture with assorted leaf shapes, sizes and tones. The result is cool, restful, interesting and inviting.

Despite its lush appearance, this garden is not demanding of water or maintenance. However, well-mulched soil and protection from hot dry winds and baking sun is essential, achieved with large screening shrubs or trees as border plantings.

Soil is richly mulched twice a year with fine bark chips to maintain moisture. Move the plants aside to spread mulch on the soil surface, but leave the area around the stems clear. Blood and bone or pelleted poultry manure is applied to the soil underneath each mulching. A good nutrient supply is essential for leafy growth. Liquid fertiliser high in nitrogen can be added every two months to boost leaf cover. Keep the garden looking attractive by picking off any burnt or damaged leaves, and trimming to tidy. Paths can become slippery with moss in conditions like these so choose anti-slip pavers. ❧

GARDEN SUMMARY

aspect sheltered sun   **climate** tropical or subtropical   **soil** well drained and mulched
water to provide a moist environment   **photographed in** summer
maintenance medium

---

1 SONG OF INDIA
Pleomele reflexa
Wonderfully leafy boughs like plumed feather dusters deck this tropical variegated shrub. It enjoys warm, humid conditions and good sunlight for maximum colour to its cream streaking.

2 JAPANESE SAGO PALM
Cycas revoluta
This very palm-like fern is a primitive remnant of ancient vegetation. It grows very slowly with a topknot of dark green fronds that can be 2m long, and develops a trunk and extending branches. A collection of several different-sized plants makes a good display, as seen here.

3 RICE-PAPER PLANT
Tetrapanax papyriferus
Large lobed leaves make this a dramatic plant. It grows stems that reach 3m in a very short time and in autumn has large sprays of creamy-white flowers. The buds, undersurface of the leaves and the stems are wrapped in cream-coloured "felt". It can cope in shade or sun so can be a useful screener, but make sure you don't plant it in a windy position or it will start to look tatty. Its suckers can be invasive.

4 ARTILLERY PLANT
Pilea microphylla
Tiny leaves in fern-like sprays cover this short-lived perennial. Each plant spreads to about 30cm, so if you want a massed effect, plant at 20cm intervals. Tiny flowers in summer fire out the pollen. Grow cuttings for replacement plants every couple of years. Fern species could be used as alternatives, but will demand more work than this easy-care plant.

5 ALTERNANTHERA
Alternanthera ficoidea
Beautiful grey-green foliage gives this low spreading plant great drama and restraint in this scene, contrasting well with its neighbours. Plant at 20cm intervals and give controlling trims when it extends too far.

The garden beyond has a border of *Alternanthera ficoidea* 'Amoena' with red, yellow and orange-streaked leaves.

Bromeliads of different varieties are used for contrasting leaf shape throughout the garden, producing occasional flower spikes in the greenscape. When they get too bulky, divide them, and nestle divisions into free draining mulch.

THE GARDEN WALL

Simplicity achieves great style in this walled courtyard design. The rich wall colour is a perfect foil to the dark green foliage of three contrasting shapes.

The scene will remain much the same throughout the year, as all three plants are evergreen and their flowers are subtle. The angle of the sun and its shadows will mark the seasons.

Pelleted poultry manure or complete plant food in spring and autumn under a thick mulch of fine bark chips will keep small pockets of soil around paved areas well fed to maintain star performers. A sprinkler system will keep the plants lush. ❧

GARDEN SUMMARY

aspect half a day's sun   **climate** temperate, Mediterranean, or subtropical
soil well nourished and mulched   **water** frequent   **photographed in** summer
maintenance low

1 LOQUAT

Eriobotrya japonica
This tree has long crinkled leaves on dark branches and produces dense shade from its round canopy. Branches can be trimmed to shape. It flowers in late autumn and fruit ripens in late winter when birds, fruit fly and jam makers race each other to it. The plant is frost- and drought-tolerant.

2 VIBURNUM

Viburnum odoratissimum
Winter clusters of white blossom are somewhat obscured but fragrant, as the name implies. The thick glossy oval leaves of this species are less susceptible to red spider mite leaf damage than other viburnum.

3 LOMANDRA

Lomandra hystrix
Soft ribbon leaves with a satiny gloss mark this grass form. It likes moist roots to keep it lush. The leaves look beautiful against the terracotta coloured wall in this confined space. They move gently in the breeze and in spring send up creamy scented flower spikes. Remove damaged leaves to keep it looking lush.

PHOTO: LEIGH CLAPP. DESIGNED BY PETER NIXON, NSW, AUSTRALIA

WATER-WISE COTTAGE GARDEN

This mass planted driveway is deceptively casual and provides interest throughout the year. New growth of re-seeded annuals and pruned perennials emerges in spring among rockery bulbs. The growth will quickly cover the fading bulb leaves with the grey of Russian sage, catmint, spurge and rock rose predominating. The grass, Stipa, makes a fine linear statement with swaying threadlike leaves.

Early summer produces the scene we have here with the purples of catmint and sea holly and the lime yellow of spurge, giving way to the pink and white of seaside daisy, grass flowers and rock rose. Winter brings its own tints as skeleton flowers and leaves are hit by frosts. Prune back in early spring or earlier if you like.

The garden is in full sun and is actually growing in gravel. Mulch added each winter will provide nutrients and bulk to the soil. These plants will thrive in a temperate or Mediterranean climate.

GARDEN SUMMARY

aspect full sun **climate** Mediterranean or temperate **soil** free draining
water undemanding **photographed in** early summer **maintenance** medium

---

1 RUSSIAN SAGE

Perovskia atriplicifolia
This grey-leafed perennial produces many woody stems growing to 30 or 50cm. They are topped in summer by small lavender-like, branching flower heads, producing a cloud-like effect. Trim back stems to ground level at the end of the season. Leave it to multiply for several years before lifting and dividing to rejuvenate the clump.

2 CATMINT

Nepeta 'Six Hills Giant'
The small grey leaves of this perennial form a mounding clump up to 1m round. In early summer, flower spikes, opening purple-blue, emerge standing well above the foliage. Tidy wandering stems and trim off faded flowers. Catmint may flower again in autumn. It does not like humidity or wet feet.

3 SEA HOLLY

Eryngium bourgatii
Grey-green spiky leaves send up branched purple stems with purple spiky-edged conical tops on this perennial. Tiny flowers are tucked into the cone. Trim back hard in spring. There is a taller form on the left.

4 SPURGE

Euphorbia polychroma
There are many forms of *Euphorbia* in this colouring. Flat heads of flowers emerge in late spring or summer. Prune back perennials and reposition seedlings for accents as required.

5 SEASIDE DAISY

Erigeron karvinskianus
This low clumping daisy has tiny white flowers that age to pink. They will seed themselves but will need tidying trims.

6 ROCK ROSE

Cistus sp.
This shrubby clamberer can drape, climb and interweave. It can also be clipped regularly to a neat 1m round. Don't prune savagely as it cannot grow from woody stems. A succession of flowers which only last a day, open through spring and summer.

7 STIPA

Stipa verticillata
A tuft-forming grass with thin foliage and spikes of flowers during summer. Cut off finished heads in spring.

DRY
CLIMATE
ROCKERY

This dramatic rocky slope has been planted with a collection of proteas and leucadendrons to create a stunning display in late winter.

Throughout the year, leaf colour or flowers or contrasting plant shapes provide a feature in the scene.

Both proteas and leucadendrons have their origins in South Africa, have been extensively cultivated, and are now grown world-wide for the cut flower trade and as accent plants for home gardens. For successful growth and maximum colour they need full sun, and to prevent the development of fungal diseases on the downy leaves, they need an environment with free movement of dry air, not fog or humidity. They also need fast draining soil, so roots do not remain wet. They do not appreciate disturbance around their roots and like a cool root run, so mulch heavily or surround them with rocks.

A soil of coarse sand mixed with large-particled bark chips, secured by rocks on sloping ground will provide appropriate conditions, even, as a last resort, over clay, as long as there is enough depth for planting and for roots to extend as they grow. They prefer slightly acid soil.

They will need once weekly watering in the first six months, and protection from frosts for the first year at least. Some are more able to withstand frosts than others, so seek information from your local nursery. Once established they don't need watering unless conditions are very dry. All are excellent cut flowers and still look good after the water has dried in the vase, so can be kept for dry arrangements as well. Cut the flower stems down low as a method of pruning. Prune off any remaining stems as flowers fade, trimming off one-third of the growth after each flowering season. ∿

GARDEN SUMMARY

aspect full sun **climate** temperate, subtropical or Mediterranean **soil** free draining, slightly acid **water** to establish **photographed in** winter **maintenance** low

PHOTO: JAIME PLAZA. PICTURED AT MT TOMAH BOTANIC GARDENS, NSW, AUSTRALIA

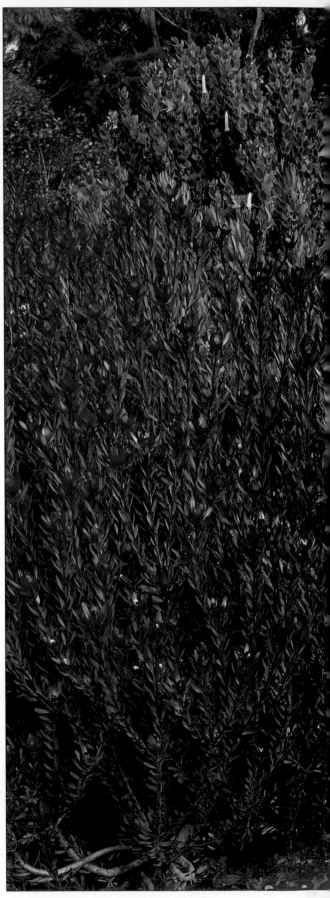

LEUCADENDRON

A large group of fast-growing evergreen shrubs and trees that modify the leaves on each stem end to attract pollinators. These modifications are called bracts and they come in a wide range of colours. Female "flowers" have cone-like centres to the bracts with tiny flowers inside. Male "flowers" are flatter cones. Pruning after flowering ensures more flowers next season.

1 *Leucadendron* 'Safari Sunset'
Two bushes here with their fabulous orange-red bracts and traces of red apparently trickling down the stems. The display lasts two to three months. The shrub grows into a roundish shape about 1m wide and 1m tall.

2 *Leaucadendron* 'Harvest'
Densely covered with its golden coat of blossoms, it can grow 50cm high by 1m across. Foliage is small and smooth green-grey on maroon stems, making it attractive year round.

3 *Leucadendron* 'Sundance'
With wine-red colouring to the lower leaves and bright gold bracts, this leucadendron has a more open shape than the others seen here, giving the garden another contrast. A tidying prune after bracts fade will keep it about 70cm tall with a similar width.

PROTEA

A collection of shrubs with a variety of heights, growth habits and leaf shapes, proteas produce large and dramatic flowers each year. The flower bracts are downy and the central complex flower cone is soft and spongy.

4 *Protea aurea* subspecies *potsbergensis*
Spoon-shaped grey-green leaves wrap the many stems. Cream outer bracts open to reveal fine cream inner ones around its tufted interior. It flowers through late summer, and is pruned back by about one third after the flowers collapse.

5 *Protea lorifolia*
Dramatic grey foliage will be topped with salmon-pink to cream flowers in late spring through to autumn. It can grow to 2.5m.

6 *Protea aristata*
Needle-like leaves are a good contrast in this group. In spring the upright cylinder bracts in deep pink surround a pink central cone.

7 *Protea nitida*
Strong green foliage and green flowers in autumn make this a dramatic feature in the garden and give an interesting contrast to the other plants.

8 *Protea compacta* hybrid
The last few flowers are seen here on a display that lasted right through autumn. It can grow to nearly 3m but needs to be pruned during its early growth stages to encourage new flower stems, and once it's fully grown, to maintain its shape.

GARDEN FEATURES

Decorative structures provide a "well dressed" look to a garden, as long as they are to scale in the scene. They can be functional or purely ornamental, but should always be used sparingly to enhance the plantings, not overwhelm them.

▲ WATER FEATURES

Pools, ponds and fountains can provide sound, cooling effect and a central feature in any garden, as long as they are scaled to suit their site. This small pool and fountain are perfect in a neat enclosed courtyard. Often pools are used as reflecting surfaces but here the growth of small duck weed provides a green contrast to surrounding brickwork.

◄ FEATURE WALLS

Gardens can be screened, divided or framed by walls, whether constructed of sticks, bricks, timber or stone. They become an essential part of the garden when dressed with plants like the roses used here, and give promise of more delights to follow with the open gate decorated with a cherub head.

▲ PERGOLA

In grand style these vine-encrusted stout pillars and beams form a backdrop to an abundant flower garden and delineate the walk. The vine is virginia creeper, *Parthenocissus tricuspidata*, which will turn red and gold in autumn, just in time to serve as a brilliant background to the second flush of roses.

BIRD BATH ►

A garden corner becomes a feature with the placement of a generous-sized birdbath among surrounding trees. Light and leaves reflect on its surface when the birds are not drinking or bathing. No doubt they are wary of the waiting cat. Terracotta pots are both practical and decorative but must be large enough to make a statement.

PHOTO: LEIGH CLAPP

THE ESCAPING GARDEN

The lawn has a foaming edge of lady's mantle, backed by stalks of Jerusalem sage, with spires of foxglove arranged casually along the border. Escapees stalk off up the hill. Structured formality flows into natural grassland beyond.

*T*ake care; make sure your escapees can be controlled and won't become weeds in the wild. This planting is for cool, rich, moist soils in morning sun. Alternatives are given to suit other climate conditions. ❧

GARDEN SUMMARY

aspect sunny **climate** temperate **soil** rich, moist, cool **water** sufficient for above
photographed in summer **maintenance** low

---

1 LADY'S MANTLE
Alchemilla mollis
This ground cover has round furry leaves that hold raindrop jewels. Summer flower stems stand above the leaves with sprays of tiny yellow flowers. Plant at 20cm intervals. Trim to tidy. Mulch over winter. Try *Anthemis* cultivars or everlastings in dry zones and brachyscomes or *Helichrysum petiolare* 'Aureum' in humidity.

2 JERUSALEM SAGE
Phlomis fruticosa
Yellow warm-season blooms arrange themselves in clusters up the stem on this shrubby perennial. Plant a staggered row 50cm apart in autumn. Trim to tidy after flowering. They tolerate limited water. In humid areas try *Pachystachys lutea*.

3 FOXGLOVES
Digitalis purpurea
The spacing of the planting along the back of the bed implies the casualness of natural re-seeding. Position well-established seedlings in groups of two or three about 50cm apart, leaving about 2 metres between groups. Plant up the hill and protect from snails, livestock and drought. Low growing wattles like *Acacia iteaphylla*, kangaroo paw, large grasses like the gahnias, and bulbs like *Crinum pedunculatum* could be "natural" escapees.

ELEGANCE IN GREY AND WHITE

There's nothing like a large established garden ornament, such as this weathered urn, to give a garden formality and structure. It sets the stage, the plants are merely players. The players here are grey-leafed hen and chickens generously overflowing the rim, a white lavender upright in the centre and repeated at the base, with additional touches that carry the theme to the backdrop. Simple yet elegant, casual yet structured, formal yet natural.

This garden is pictured in summer, in the early morning light. As sun fills the garden most of the day, these sun loving plants were selected. Grey-leafed plants will grow pale and leggy if struggling to reach sunlight and succulents will lose their colour. They all have modified their leaves to enable them to survive drought conditions so will need little maintenance watering. They will however, need maintenance trimming. Soil should be free-draining but well mulched in the surrounding gardens, and given a feed at least once a year with pelleted poultry manure or complete plant food. See the note below in hen and chickens entry about soil for the urn. Size and placement of an urn like this are important details. Scale down or up to suit your site. The climate here is temperate, but these plantings are also suitable for Mediterranean and cool subtropical conditions.

GARDEN SUMMARY

aspect full sun   **climate** Mediterranean or temperate   **soil** well drained light to rich
water only during very dry spells   **photographed in** summer   **maintenance** medium

---

1 LAVENDER
Lavandula species white
Place well-grown cuttings or plants 50cm apart in full sun. Buy an extra one or two for the urn. Nip out tops to develop side shoots. Flowers emerge in late spring or summer. Trim after flowering and in late autumn to maintain bushy shape. If humidity is a problem try *Helichrysum petiolare*.

2 HEN AND CHICKENS
Echeveria spp
Make sure drainage holes are clear in urn, fill base with small gravel or stones to a level above the holes, then top with good quality potting mix. The water must drain away and not pool. Plant several rosettes of good grey-coloured hen and chickens at 20cm intervals around the edge, and a centre circle 10cm from these. Position the lavender in the centre with a scoop of slow release fertiliser.

3 LAMBS EARS
Stachys byzantina
Soft furry leaves give this plant its name. Place single plants 25cm apart. They produce soft blue flower spikes in late summer. Trim them after flowering, or before, if flowers are unwanted. In humidity try *Plectranthus argentatus*.

4 PLUMBAGO
Plumbago auriculata alba
Generous and exuberant, plumbago grows into a dense thicket and decks itself with phlox-like flowers during the warm months. It's a great screener and is seen here in its white form. Position plants 1m apart in at least half a day sunlight (here partly shaded in summer by an alder, *Alnus* sp). A single plant can spread to 2m by 2m. Prune in autumn or early spring.

5 ORANGE JESSAMINE
Murraya paniculata
This dark green shiny-leafed shrub starts innocently as a neat round, usually planted at 1m intervals. Be prepared for it to grow treelike to 5m high by 3m wide. It responds well to regular trimming rather than a once-a-year pruning. Flushes of sweetly perfumed white flower clusters occur during the warm months.

PHOTO: LEIGH CLAPP. DESIGNED BY GARDEN IMPRESSIONS, NSW, AUSTRALIA

PHOTO: LEIGH CLAPP. DESIGNED BY GARDEN IMPRESSIONS, NSW, AUSTRALIA

THE FRONT GARDEN

*A formal Federation-style house
with an asymmetrical front has
a garden dressed in similar style,
with softened formality, old
fashioned plants (or their modern
improved cultivars) and
asymmetrical but linked gardens.*

Neat and trim around the entry are
shaped box and star jasmine. But
elsewhere by way of contrast are
exuberant climbers up the walls, flowering
mounds among the flagstones, wandering
ground covers and mixed mass plantings.
More contrast is provided with one side
grassy, the other paved and "urned".
Shrubs and the next door jacaranda screen
the garden from neighbours and the street.

Pictured in spring in a subtropical area,
the plants used here would also suit
Mediterranean and temperate zones.

Soil is built up twice a year with
mulchings of mushroom compost and fine
bark chips. Pelleted poultry manure or
complete plant food is added under the
mulch. The garden will need a long
soaking once a week but more during
very dry hot conditions. This planting will
provide interest year round.

GARDEN SUMMARY

aspect full sun **climate** subtropical,
temperate or Mediterranean
soil well mulched and fed
water once a week good soaking; roses may
need more **photographed in** spring
maintenance high

1 STAR JASMINE

Trachelospermum jasminoides
This abundant twining climber has dark green leaves and white perfumed flowers in spring. It winds up posts or can form cables of its stems. It can be pruned to a neat shape as seen here around the door, or let run free as it has around the windows. Trim off its triffid-like stems in summer as it can twine onto plants, trees, eaves and roofs where it's not wanted. When cut, the stems produce a white sap which can burn the skin or eyes if it comes into contact with them. Take care and wash off with quantities of water if necessary. In frosty areas try clematis for a similar exuberant display.

2 ROSES

Standard roses, used here for formality and height, are *Rosa* 'Iceberg'. They produce a succession of fragrant cluster blooms from spring to late autumn if continually trimmed back to a leaf junction about 10cm below fading flowers. They last well in vases and are beautifully perfumed. Garden roses in the front beds are *R.* 'Charles Austin' on the right, and *R.* 'The Miller' on the left. David Austin bred roses with old-fashioned looking blooms and fragrance, combined with repeat flowering generosity and disease resistance. They will need rigorous pruning or layering to keep them low. You could try *R.* 'The Fairy', *R.* 'Green Ice' or the ground cover rose, 'Apple Blossom' as low-growing alternatives, providing less pruning tasks but a good cover of blossom. Little perfume, alas.

3 LAVENDER

Lavandula dentata and *L. angustifolia*
Small neat grey-leafed accents are used as contrasts. Try *L. dentata*, French lavender, which bears blue flower heads almost all year in subtropical zones. It may succumb to heavy frost in temperate areas. The summer flowering *L. angustifolia*, English lavender, will be more reliable in cool areas. Lavender always looks beautiful with roses and helps obscure the rose's bareness in winter. In the

urn is a neat round *L.* 'Munstead Dwarf', which flowers in summer. Always keep lavender well trimmed to prevent woody growth spoiling the grey-leafed compactness. Both leaves and flowers can be dried for potpourri.

4 BOX HEDGE

Buxus japonica
These clipped small-leafed box trees give a neat formality. Start with plants no more than 20cm high and plant them 10cm apart along the edge of the path. Trim them regularly even though they are still growing, to keep them leafy. Once they have reached their planned height continue maintenance trimming. See page 7 for shaping and trimming information. The curved sweep to the steps forms an inviting entry frame. As an alternative consider a wire frame with entwined climbers like ivy or *Muehlenbeckia*, but keep in mind that these will require regular trimming of outreaching stems. They can become invasive and suffocate other plants.

5 CHERRY PIE

Heliotropium arborescens
The light mauve flowering form is used here. Its leaves have a purplish hue all year and tone well with the lavender. There is a lime-yellow-leafed form also and another with deep purple flowers. All would fit well in this scheme. The flowers are sweetly perfumed and provide the plant's common name. Clip off deadheads and wayward branches as they do tend to sprawl.

6 GARDENIA

Gardenia augusta 'Florida'
It has dark glossy leaves, stems topped with white perfumed flowers in spring, and if you're lucky, it will spot flower until autumn. Pick off flowers as they start to yellow to keep up appearances and encourage more blooms. Watch out for black sooty mould caused by round brown scale insects attached to stems and leaves, they weaken the plant and reduce flowers. Pick or brush them off with soapy water and a toothbrush. This plant does not tolerate frosts; try japonica *Chaenomeles speciosa* or

Magnolia stellata as white-flowered alternatives in frosty areas. As well as being attractive, their early flowers are delightful harbingers of spring.

7 WINDFLOWERS

Anemone x *hybrida*
Attractive velvety divided leaves clothe this perennial all year. In late summer/autumn, spikes up to 1m tall, with a candelabra of buds emerge, opening as a slightly cupped flower with many prominent stamens. Their pink, carmine or white flowers can be double or single, the choice is up to you. Plant a cluster of two or three, spaced 50cm apart, in part shade. Keep moist until established. They will form clumps that can be divided every few years.

8 SALVIA

Salvia 'Indigo Spires'
This purple-flowered perennial salvia can reach 1.5m high and wide. Plant it in full sun or at least six hours' sunlight for compact growth. It will bloom from late spring right through to autumn. Regularly trim off spent flowers to encourage more and to control its shape. Prune it back hard in late winter or early spring. It is frost-hardy.

9 TOBACCO FLOWER

Nicotiana hybrids
Plant as seedlings in late winter/early spring, selecting colours to suit your scheme. White, lime-yellow, pink and carmine forms are available. Large tobacco-like leaves develop (it is a relative) and a tall spire of buds emerges in six to eight weeks. Flowers are delicately perfumed. Use in vases or trim spent blooms to extend flowering time. They can self-seed.

10 LAMIUM

Lamium 'White Nancy'
Use this cultivar, and not the far more invasive aluminium plant. The white leaf centres feature all year and white flowers appear in spring and summer. It does well in sun or part shade and will quickly cover 50cm but it will need tidying trims. New plants can be developed from rooted runners.

11 CHINESE FORGET-ME-NOT

Cynoglossum amabile

There are rich blue dashes of colour
among the green and grey foliage of
this pretty cottage plant which grows
spires of flowers 50cm tall. The basal
leaf clumps are broad greenish-grey
leaves expanding to 30cm. They grow
happily in between flagstones and can
easily re-seed and develop in small
cracks and crevices in paths. Move
these to positions you want. Both white
and blue forms are available and both
will suit a scheme like this. Planted in
early spring, they will flower and re-seed
for the next year's show in spring and
summer. They don't mind frost.

12 SWEET ALYSSUM

Lobularia maritima

Put seed or seedlings among the flagstones in early spring right through to
autumn for a pretty dappled effect.

They will flower densely but will
eventually become leggy. Trim back or
replace to tidy. Self-sown seedlings will
also establish themselves, so watch
out for them coming up in the garden
and transplant to the position you want.
White, pink-white and cream coloured
varieties are available.

13 SEASIDE DAISY

Erigeron karvinskianus

Dainty little pink and white daisies are
used to soften edges and fill in gaps.
Plant where needed and trim to tidy
during summer. They will become
clumped over dead understems that
should be removed. They will usually
self-seed.

14 GROUND MORNING GLORY

Convolvulus sabatius

This form is said to be more upright
than the cascading *C. mauritanicus*. It

has fine trailing stems and grey-green
leaves with purple trumpet flowers
during the warm months. Individual
plants will spread about 50cm.

15 LAMBS EARS

Stachys byzantina

Generous spreads of furry grey "ears"
are used as a foreground planting. Pale
blue spires of flowers appear in
summer. Plant one to fill 50cm by the
end of summer. Trim off dead leaves
and leggy shoots and use suckers to
replace old clumps.

16 GOLDEN OREGANO

Origanum vulgare 'Aureum'

Grown principally for its summer gold,
this herb will sucker and can spread
greedily at the expense of others, so
keep it trimmed. Don't be disappointed
by its winter green; with summer
warmth the yellow returns.

HANGING BASKET ▶

This generously planted hanging basket has been carefully arranged so that cascades of leaf and flower colour will continue through spring and into summer. Feed regularly and water every day or attach a drip watering system to maintain moisture. Hang in a bright position out of direct sun and protect from winds for a successful display. Lobelia climbs and falls; a fuchsia drapes with its bells; yellow leaves of creeping jenny, *Lysimachia nummularia* 'Aurea', provide contrast and dainty white and pink seaside daisy, *Erigeron karvinskianus*, fill in the gaps.

▲ AFRICAN VIOLET

A simple arrangement using two forms of the same coloured African violet, *Saintpaulia ionantha*, planted among rocks for a dramatic contrast. This can be brought indoors and placed in good light or grown outside under protective awnings or eaves.

LONG LASTING ▶

Demonstrating how important pot choice is when planning to make a feature is this delightful weathered terracotta urn simply planted with a Japanese maple. Winter bareness could be used to display early spring bulbs around the trunk before the leaves unfurl.

WINTER DISPLAY ▶

A pretty arrangement of jonquils, *Narcissus* 'Erlicheer' and supporting pots of johnny-jump-u+9ps or heartsease, *Viola tricolor*, have been arranged (one of the beauties of potted plants), in sunlight under a mauve flowering hovea. Planting bulbs in pots is a wonderful way to display them but does require special treatment. Refer to bulb planting information on their packets.

THE POTTED GARDEN

Arranging plants in pots is rather like arranging flowers in a vase, except that the plants must grow into the arrangement. Nature does what it does and there will often be interesting surprises in colour arrangements and growth patterns. It is essential to use a good grade of potting mix and suitable pots and to feed every two weeks with liquid fertiliser for lush growth during warm months. Tidying trims are usually necessary to keep these accent pieces at their best.

VEGETABLE GARDEN ▶

Vegetables can look magnificent in a pot as well as being practical. Here a mix of lettuce varieties are teamed with purple basil. Fed and watered regularly they will be a feast to the eyes and supply you with mixed salad greens over several weeks. Start a new collection every month. Beans, tomatoes, cucumbers, zucchini, in fact most vegetables will adjust or have been bred for pot culture.

EASY CARE ▶

Cacti of mixed shape and size can happily be grouped like this to create dramatic impact and are easy to care for. Very free draining mix, very good light and very little water will ensure success. They come in a startling range of shapes: some round, some columns, some sticklike, some with very broad leaves and some looking just like pebbles. Select a collection to suit your pot, but do handle them with care as their spines can cause painful wounds. Flowering time depends on the varieties chosen and their age, but it is possible to have flowers almost year round.

PHOTO: LEIGH CLAPP. DESIGNED BY PENNY RUDDUCK, SA, AUSTRALIA

THE SHADY GLADE

This shady glade is a Mediterranean garden
dressed jewel bright with assorted leaf colour,
the accent on green and purple with highlights of cream.
Dropped autumn leaves add an interesting contrast
and provide mulch.

The tree filters the hot summer sun and there is additional shade cast by buildings, walls and surrounding trees. There are many positions in gardens where these conditions prevail: side paths, courtyards, entry courts and under trees. This is definitely not a full sun planting.

The soil is supporting trees, vines, palms and densely planted ground cover specimens so must be frequently fed. Four times a year sprinkle with slow release pelleted poultry manure, making sure that it comes into contact with the soil. Cover with a thick layer of garden compost or spent mushroom compost, to reduce the odour and double the benefit to the garden. Nitrogen-rich fertiliser is essential for luxuriant leaf growth.

The tropical look is partly dependant on adequate water and slow draining soil, and this is where the generous mulching pays dividends. The shade will reduce water demands and the hardy species used here will only require a good soaking once a week in dry weather. Plants have been suggested for different climate zones. ❧

GARDEN SUMMARY

aspect shaded for more than half a day   **climate** Mediterranean   **soil** rich, slow draining   **watering** deep soaking once a week   **photographed in** autumn
maintenance high

---

1 MANCHURIAN PEAR

Pyrus ussuriensis
This deciduous tree grows to about 7m, its rounded glossy leaves turning yellow to red in autumn. Its spring blossoms are clusters of tiny white flowers which develop into small hard yellowish fruit which are ornamental, not edible. It is happy in both subtropical mild winters and cooler climate frosts, but needs good deep watering to prevent the leaves from shrivelling around their edges.

2 STAR JASMINE

Trachelospermum jasminoides
A delightfully obliging evergreen vine, star jasmine will cover a fence or screen in a year in most climate zones. The white five-petalled flowers are sweetly fragrant. They appear in spring and can completely obscure the dark green leaves. Long, twining tendrils may need a controlling trim to prevent the vine draping itself too far. Beware of the milky sap, it can sting the skin and burn the eyes.

3 CYCAD

Macrozamia communis or *Cycas revoluta*
Both these plants have similar palm-like foliage. The *Cycas* will tolerate frosts and is generally very hardy, whereas the *Macrozamia* needs frost-free conditions. They both grow very slowly, so select one that has enough height to fill the position.

4 MOTHER-IN-LAWS TONGUE

Sansevieria trifasciata 'Laurentii'
The cultivar used here has clear cream edges with grey and green horizontal central markings. It will clump and when it is too large, it can be divided to make new plantings. Pooling water can cause the roots to rot so make sure the soil is well-drained. There is a frost-tolerant form, or replace with aspidistra, the cast iron plant.

5 CALATHEA

Calathea cultivar
Buy plants with strong markings for dramatic effect. They will spread to a clump 80cm to 1m if given humidity and humus-rich soil. Where there is frost, substitute hostas, which will give a luxuriant summer display, die back in winter and return again in the warm. The violets will spill over during winter to cover gaps.

6 & 7 PLECTRANTHUS

Two species are used here. The furry grey-leafed form is *Plectranthus argentatus* with some of its mauve flower heads still present. The green plant with the cream edge is *P. madagascariensis*. They both have meandering lax stems that will lean on their neighbours for support or fall to the ground and set down roots there. It is very easy to trim off leggy growth and these trimmings can be used as cuttings for new plants. Both this and coleus as an alternative will not stand frost. Purple and green flowering hellebores would make an adequate cold climate substitute.

8 CORDYLINE

Cordyline australis 'Rubra'
Wonderful accent points here with its purple colouring and fine strappy leaves. They are not demanding but are slow growing, so buy two of different heights for contrast when doing the initial planting. When too tall, prune off as described for dracaena.

9 DRACAENA

Dracaena deremensis 'Purpurea'
More fabulous purple accent from this broader-leafed form with a green and purple form growing nearby. They can become lanky with age, but can be cut back and the top shoots started as a replacement of the right height. Frost can burn them.

10 MOSES IN THE BASKET

Tradescantia spathacea
A rosette of greenish purple leaves up to 30cm long form the "basket" where "Moses", a little white flower, is cradled. Spreading much more gently than wandering jew, its cousin, the clumps can easily be removed and replanted as needed. Purple ajuga might substitute in frosty areas, with a light mulch protection.

11 MONDO GRASS

Ophiopogon planiscapus 'Nigrescens'
Touches of this purple-leafed grass are tucked in to add strappy forms to the front. Less aggressive a spreader than the green form, it will still need some control by division.

12 LILY TURF

Liriope muscari 'Variegata'
Used here as an accent clump, the cream-striped leaf brings light to the foreground. Mauve-blue flowers appear in summer. The clump will increase in size and may need division to refresh and control.

13 VIOLETS

Viola odorata
Clumping ground cover violets look green and cushiony all year through and will flower in semi-shade in winter. They spread by underground roots and seed so may need to be controlled. There are some purple-leafed varieties.

14 SUCCULENTS

Odd dots of grey-leafed succulents have been used as accents and space-fillers. Select shapes and heights to suit your display and that will thrive in your conditions. Many succulents are not frost-tolerant.

STREET GARDEN

The wrought iron fence, barbed with arrow heads, protects the house from the nearby street. A gum tree grows in the narrow front garden. Softening detail is supplied by flowers twining through the bars in this summer display.

These showy annuals need full sun and well drained soil. For maximum effect, it is essential to break up the soil before each planting, and to add complete plant food and old cow manure, spent mushroom or garden compost. Deeply mulch with fine bark chips. Rest it for two weeks.

Plant summer flowering seedlings in spring, moving mulch aside to place them 10cm apart. Water well. To encourage bulky growth and hence more flowers, nip out each central bud. Plant lobelia at the front and back and petunias in the centre producing a sea of blue with central white "mountains".

This display will last through summer but remove it before it becomes ragged. Treat the soil once more, let it rest, then plant the winter/spring display. Suggested plantings to repeat the colour arrangement are white primula and blue viola. For a change of scene try Iceland poppies with yellow-toned violas or wallflowers and linaria. Plant these in autumn.

PETUNIA
Petunia hybrids
They are usually sold in colour-named punnets, so select carefully when. designing your display. Nip out centres to trim leggy growth. They make an interesting small vase detail and last well.

LOBELIA
Lobelia hybrids
Again, colour mixes or single colours available. Trim off regularly to encourage regrowth and prevent an accumulation of dead woody growth underneath.

GARDEN SUMMARY

aspect full sun   **climate** temperate, Mediterranean or subtropical
soil preferably well tended   **water** once or twice a week once established
photographed in summer   **maintenance** medium

CITY COURTYARD

The problem: summer sun but winter shade in a tiny courtyard which is viewed from,
and is an integral part of, the house, but is overviewed by neighbours.
The answer: lightly screen it with a translucent fence,
wrap it in greenery and create a focus.

Here the owners have used a stick fence which lets light and air move through but contains the view. Twiggy greenery traced against it reduces the hard surface and adds more screen. Abundant shade-tolerant plantings at the base brighten the scene and accent the focus, which, at this time, is the lily and the rest of the year is the urn in good light atop a column.

The soil has been brought in to fill narrow beds at the edge of the paving. Nutrients must be available to the plants in such confined situations. Slow release chemical fertilisers work well and because they are odourless are probably best here, but they must be reapplied regularly. Mulch over the top. All of these plants can be grown in pots should the courtyard be soil-less. The height of the urn allows winter sun to shine on the orchid there, just when it needs it. Remember to give it fertiliser also. ❧

GARDEN SUMMARY

aspect semi-shade   **climate** subtropical, temperate or Mediterranean
soil well mulched and regularly fertilised   **water** frequent but light
photographed in spring   **maintenance** low

1 HIBISCUS

Hibiscus rosa-sinensis
Planted here for summer flowers, the hibiscus is struggling in the shade. A winter-flowering camellia or twining summer-flowering mandevilla or hoya might be more successful.

2 CAMELLIA

Camellia sasanqua
This small-leafed camellia is tolerant of some shade and puts on a good show of flowers in autumn. To keep it small, tip prune it regularly (except when flower buds are developing) and woody ends won't be visible.

3 AZALEA

Azalea kurume
A small-leafed azalea, the kurume is covered with a mass of small flowers in spring. Azaleas are notorious for leaf and flower problems, but plant them if you don't mind the challenge. Fuchsias or the unusual *Breynia disticha* 'Roseo-picta' could make a less troublesome but still interesting effect.

4 GREEN GODDESS LILY

Zantedeschia aethiopica 'Green Goddess'
A generous display of green-splotched white lilies make a feature of this plant in spring. The flowers last a long time in vases, but if left on the plant they develop dramatic seed heads. Plant in winter and let them develop into a lush clump of greenery for a few years before dividing them. They like partial shade and damp soil. Trim off decaying leaves and finished seed heads.

5 BUSY LIZZIES

Impatiens cultivars
Everyone's favourite shade plant, little faces of bright colour liven up the gloom. You can select colour, height and flower form to suit, or collect cuttings from friends and grow your own. Once planted you'll have them forever, as long as it's a bit damp. Be warned, they easily get out of control.

6 SLIPPER ORCHID

Paphiopedilum species
This small-leafed orchid forms a clump of greenery all year, comes into bud during autumn and flowers in late winter for a long-lasting display. It won't cope with frost, but a cymbidium orchid will. Orchids look wonderful displayed in a raised position such as this — it's the best way to show off their cascading blooms. Make sure the potting mix is well drained, and feed after flowering.

FLOWERING ORCHARD

A garden orchard can be pretty, low maintenance, inviting and bountiful. All it needs is a bit of decorative planting and simple garden treatments. The fruit trees will benefit from the extra soil care while the underplanting enjoys the dappled summer sun and winter brightness.

The owners of this inviting garden get a pleasant area to view, roam in and gather produce from. This is a temperate garden with spring blossom still on the apple trees, and the last of the bulbs fading.

The soil, rich and slow draining, should be well tended if the fruit trees are to produce, however deep digging around the root zone (under the tree canopy) is not recommended. Lightly tease the soil if compacted, spread pelleted poultry manure then mulch over with spent mushroom compost, garden compost or manure. Let the worms take it down through the soil. Repeat the process each autumn or early spring.

Fruit trees will need long soaking watering in hot dry spells, the flowers will be happy with the leftovers. ⌒

GARDEN SUMMARY

aspect full sun **climate** temperate **soil** rich, slow draining **water** generous
photographed in spring **maintenance** low

---

1 APPLE
Malus spp
Select two or more varieties that produce well in your area and that will ripen at different times. Plant 3m to 5m apart. Keep well watered, mulched and fed. Prune to shape during winter. Other fruit trees for this environment include plum, peach, cherry, or quince.

2 FORGET-ME-NOT
Myosotis alpestris
Forget-me-not runs rampant. It will seed and reproduce the effect as long as it's allowed. Establish by spot planting at 15cm intervals in early spring.

3 COLUMBINE
Aquilegia x *hybrida*
Colombines love partial shade and moist conditions and will self-seed. Grey divided leaves send up a spire of buds, opening as coppery- and mauve-toned nodding bells in spring.

4 BULBS
The flowers have finished on daffodils, jonquils and bluebells and only their leaves remain. They were in full sun during leafless winter and made bright splashes as they flowered. For bulb planting details see page 8. To establish under existing trees, break into the root zone with a mattock in only a few positions per tree, add composted manure and slow release fertiliser and position the bulbs in the pockets. Mulch deeply over the top. With tree roots competing for nutrients it is essential to feed and mulch each autumn. They will then become clumps.

5 IRIS
Iris germanica
Sword leaves of iris look dramatic at any time of year. In spring they are crowned with heads of flowers. Make sure they are planted where they can bake in the sun.

6 ROSES
Rosa species
Roses, looking healthy but not floriferous in the shade, were probably planted when the trees were small. Tepees of perennial sweet peas, snow peas, shrubby hydrangeas or spires of foxglove could perform better.

Potted colour is provided by *Viola* x *wittrockiana* or primula.

Subtropical and tropical zones can grow citrus, avocado, pawpaw, mango as suitable, with coleus, plectranthus, violet or busy lizzie underplantings. Mediterranean areas could grow olive, almond, fig or apricot with violet or vinca and forget-me-not spread under.

PHOTO: LEIGH CLAPP. PICTURED AT RED COW FARM. NSW. AUSTRALIA

COTTAGE FRONT GARDEN

This entry framework charmingly dresses a symmetrical unadorned cottage. The exuberance of the rose-filled veranda and frivolous path plantings are set off by the sombre clipped rosemary against the crisp white fence.

*T*he old fashioned plants used suit the scene perfectly. The climate is temperate or cool subtropical.

The soil here is heavy red clay, and is given a thick mulch in winter of spent mushroom, garden or leaf compost, or cow manure. Dig this in in spring, (or allow the worms to do it) and apply a good layer of fine bark mulch to retain moisture over summer. Sand or loam require the same treatment. Both the roses and rosemary will need slow release fertiliser or pelleted poultry manure at their feet under the mulch in spring, and annuals and perennials should be given a similar boost at planting or trimming time.

Maintenance includes trimming of rosemary to maintain its shape (saving stems for cooking); cutting back flower spikes of columbines, bleeding heart and spurge after seeds have dropped; and regular tidying of pinks on the path. Old fashioned roses like 'Lamarque' do not need hard pruning except for thorny stems that block access. The lower roses will need regular pruning. ∽

GARDEN SUMMARY

aspect full sun   **climate** temperate
soil slow draining   **water** generous
photographed in spring   **maintenance** high

1 ROSEMARY

Rosmarinus officinalis
This aromatic shrub can grow 1.5m
round. It needs regular trimming. Pale
blue-mauve flowers appear on stem
ends through summer.

2 PINKS

Dianthus x *allwoodii*
Pinks, as well as scenting the air,
brighten the path throughout spring and
summer with a vibrant colour mix. The
grey foliage mat softens the edges
when flowers are finished. Plant rooted
cuttings or nursery stock 30cm apart in
autumn for a spring display. Sweet
alice, catmint, brachyscome or snow-in-
summer could be substitutes in drier or
humid climates.

3 COLUMBINE

Aquilegia cultivars
Very dramatic deep purple columbines
are positioned among the roses. They
are an annual, but may take two years
to flower if planted late. They are
always attractive with their soft grey
rounded leaves. The flower spike
emerges in spring and opens with bell-
shaped blooms. Columbines die after
seeds drop and will re-seed if the soil
is damp. Reposition seedlings if
necessary. Try red-purple leafed
Pelargonium 'Leonie Holborow' in drier
or even humid conditions.

4 BLEEDING HEART

Dicentra spectabilis
A clump of fernlike leaves send out
arching stems in spring and summer,
opening as a line of pinkish red hearts
with a central drop. The deep green
leaves contrast with the grey of the
columbines and like them, need moist
conditions. Salvias or pentas could
substitute in drier or humid zones.

5 SPURGE

Euphorbia wulfenii
Lime green heads on blue-green-leafed
stems make a dramatic impact. This
shrub flowers in spring. Prune off the
finished heads to ground level so new
stems will develop for next year. Plant
as accents allowing 60cm to 80cm for
width and height. It will probably self-
seed, so move seedlings to the
positions you choose or discard them
as they emerge.

6 ROSES

Old fashioned roses are used here.
Seek out what is performing well in
your area for the effect you want.

Rosa 'Lamarque' clambers up and
drapes from the veranda supports. It
flowers profusely in spring and autumn
and has wonderful perfume. The
flowers can burn in hot sun, so don't
face it to the west. The pinks and
yellows below would have to suit your
conditions: pink *R.* 'Fantin Latour' or
'The Miller', or yellow 'Charles Austin'
perhaps in temperate conditions. Try
R. 'Lorraine Lee' or rugosas for pink
roses, and yellow 'Lady Huntingfield' in
subtropical or Mediterranean zones.

FRAGRANT FLOWERS

*The waft of a flower's fragrance can stop you in your tracks. Often the source
is shyly hidden among leaves, as with winter honeysuckle, osmanthus
and citrus blossom. Others, like roses, jasmine and frangipani
fill the air and the scene. There are perfumers that will fill your garden
every season; seek them out and fill up your senses.*

◀ HONEYSUCKLE

Honeysuckle vines are vigorous climbers that will conceal unsightly
buildings or fences and will flower in clusters in spring and summer. There
are several varieties with attractive colourings so select to suit your
scheme. However, be warned, honeysuckle is *really* vigorous and should
be pruned back to tidy in late winter. Trailing stems heading out in the
wrong direction along the ground or over its neighbours are best removed.

MAGNOLIA ▶

Deciduous magnolias
make great impact in
a garden in early
winter with their
twisted limbs and
furry buds. In late
winter or spring the
buds burst, producing
more drama, with
either tulip-shaped
blooms or flattened
stars as here with
Magnolia stellata.
Their perfume is rich
and exotic. They like
rich soil and a
protected position.

▲ LILY-OF-THE-VALLEY

A gentle green leafy carpet announces the return of lily-of-
the-valley, a perennial that dies back for the cold and
snow of winter. Sprays of perfumed bells emerge in
dappled shade under trees before leaves develop, their
scent fills the air. Their appearance guarantees the end of
winter: a genuine harbinger of spring in cold climes.

SPANISH BROOM ▶

Spanish Broom, *Spartium junceum*, stands up stiff with
leafless green stalks through winter and spring. Come
early summer it starts to dress itself in clear yellow pea-
like flowers that are sweetly lemon-scented, completely
disguising its porcupine appearance. It copes well with
wind, drought and snow.

FORMAL GARDEN

Here is an arrangement of leaf shapes and colours set in structured formality.
The effect is soothing: sunlight is dappled, textures are smooth, shapes are ordered.
There are no jarring elements. The neat topiary ball and clipped hedging
counterbalance the generosity of the lime robinia foliage above
and the lax locks of mondo grass at their feet.

This design idea could be used as a small formal garden, or as an entry court or a linking area between larger and differing garden rooms. At least four or five hours summer sun must reach these plantings to maintain their vigour. In winter, the lower angle of the sun through the bare branches of the robinia will suffice.

Soil should be mulched with compost or fine bark chips twice a year. Slow release fertiliser or pelleted poultry manure should be added at the same time, in contact with the soil under the mulch. The pot will need slow release fertiliser in spring and autumn. Watering should be sufficient to prevent the box and mondo grass looking stressed — a good soaking once a week should be enough, but in very hot weather, give the robinia extra water to prevent the leaves from scorching and to keep it lush.

This picture shows the garden in late spring/early summer, and uses plantings that would suit Mediterranean, temperate and subtropical climates. The secret to the success of this planting is repetition of plant varieties, rather than a conflict of varied shapes and forms. ❧

GARDEN SUMMARY

aspect sun for half a day   **climate** temperate, Mediterranean, or subtropical
soil well fed and mulched   **water** weekly deep soaking, extra on robinias
photographed in late spring   **maintenance** medium

1 ROBINIA

Robinia pseudoacacia 'Frisia'
The impact of its colour, size, shape and seasonal changes make it a success as a specimen, street tree, grove or an avenue, as seen here, marching off to the next garden room. It grows to about 10m in a tapering form or develops an umbrella-like canopy if pruned early at its top. White wisteria-like flowers appear in spring with the new leaves. In autumn the leaves become more golden before they fall. Roots will seek out water in broken pipes and sewers so be careful with initial placement. Thorny suckers can develop from the rootstock, remove them as soon as possible.

2 BAY

Lauris nobilis
Bay has leathery dark green leaves and dark green-grey branches. It can grow into a 12m round tree if left alone but is here used as a low pleached hedge. Planted in a row 50cm apart, their tops have been regularly trimmed off, side growth has been encouraged to entwine with its neighbours, while forward- and back-reaching branches are controlled to maintain the hedge shape. Regular trimming of thin stems after each growth spurt will prevent bare woody stems.

3 BOX

Buxus sempervirens
Box has been used here in both hedges and topiary ball. You can start the hedges as small as 10cm pot size plants, larger if the budget will allow, and position them 10cm apart. Start trimming as soon as they are planted, see page 7. Topiary balls can be bought, and only need trimming to maintain. To establish your own, buy a large plant and round it with each trim.

4 MONDO GRASS

Ophiopogon japonicus
Leathery evergreen ribbon leaves crowd from the underground stems on this grass. It masses wonderfully but can become invasive. Trim with a spade along the garden edge to neaten, and lift and divide every few years to keep it vigorous.

PHOTO: LEIGH CLAPP. DESIGNED BY GARDEN IMPRESSIONS, NSW, AUSTRALIA

SUNNY DRY SLOPE

At its most floriferous in spring as seen here, this sun-baked slope is bright with buttons of daisies; leaf colour contributes accents throughout the rest of the year — with ne'ry a cry for water. Three or four different daisy-flowering plants are massed here, their uncomplicated open faces just smiling at the sun. Hundreds of chances to make loves me, loves me not, decisions!

Some of these daisies are not happy in frost but neighbours' gardens or your nursery will have varieties on show to suit your conditions. Deep pockets of soil allow roots to grow down and the large rocks keep all in place. They also act as water retainers when moisture is drawn up and condenses on the rock surface in the cool of the night.

Complete garden fertiliser or pelleted poultry manure applied twice a year ensures vigorous growth and flowering. Composted fine bark mulch spread 3cm thick over the soil surface at fertiliser time will retain moisture and will break down slowly to add essential organic matter. Pick daisies often for arrangements, and deadhead regularly to promote strong flower growth. It is best to trim deadheads from daisies after all flower flushes, to keep the bushes looking good and maintain a compact shape, but most will become too leggy eventually and will need replacement. Gazania and ice plant can be similarly revitalised for peak performance. ❧

GARDEN SUMMARY

aspect full sun **climate** Mediterranean, temperate or subtropical
soil deep and well drained **water** minimal **photographed in** spring
maintenance low

1 MARGUERITE DAISIES
Argyranthemum frutescens
Individual shrubs will grow 1m high and round, so, unless you're mass planting, position them to allow growth to a full rounded shape. Select a variety of single and double forms and colours to suit your scheme. Trim back after flowering to lower bud clusters and remove leggy wooden stems to leaf buds. It's best to replace them at least every two years for problem-free and vigorous plants. Strike cuttings of woody stems in winter or green new growth in spring and summer and plant out where required.

2 PARIS DAISY
Euryops pectinatus
Grey-green fernlike leaves are softly downed and its yellow daisies stand out from them on stiff stems during winter and spring. Prune back to new leaf growth half way down the stem, after flowering. Shrubby white *Olearia* could also be used.

3 GAZANIA
Gazania hybrids
Gazanias can have a clump-forming or a trailing growth pattern, the leaves can be green with grey backs or entirely grey. All gazanias produce bright coloured flowers in sunny conditions throughout the warm months. The cream, pink, orange, yellow or red petals usually have a black marker line around their bases for dramatic contrast. Strike new plants from stem trimmings during summer or dig up rooted runners. They will spread out to cover half a metre.

PHOTO: GEOFFREY BURNIE. PICTURED AT OWEN HUGHES' GARDEN, TAS. AUSTRALIA

4 ORANGE BROWALLIA

Streptosolen jamesonii
Clustered small orange and yellow
trumpets cover this shrub from late
winter through spring. Prune back hard
after flowering, its neat crinkled leaves
will soon clothe it again until flowers
reappear. A white rock rose could
provide summer interest and will thrive
in these conditions.

5 ICE PLANT

Mesembryanthemum cultivars
Clumping grey-green foliage is in the
form of cylinders on this ground
covering succulent. Daisy flowers cover
the plant in spring, opening in sun and
glistening as though newly lacquered.
They close their petals when skies are
clouded. Colour choices range from
white, pinks and reds, and there are

many alternatives to flower size and
form. Trim them to tidy after flowering.

There are many other perennials that
will provide daisy-shaped flowers to suit
these conditions. Chrysanthemums,
rudbeckia, shasta daisies and
sneezeweed are examples. Annuals like
gaillardia and calendula would also be
at home in this garden.

THE WHITE GARDEN

Photographed in all its spring glory, this temperate climate garden shows how careful designing creates a stunning display. Here white flowers are supported by dashes of white-streaked and grey foliage.

*C*ool climate gardens always seem to burst exuberantly forth after the dormancy of winter, relieved to have the chance to perform again.

Cold winter and drying summer winds are screened from this area by a wonderfully dense shrub border, producing a microclimate of warmer and moister conditions. Soil type should be rich, deep and slow draining with a thick mulch of manure applied each winter. Dig it in by spring if the worms have not already done this for you. Extra organic matter is added as the spring show commences when the soil is deeply mulched with composted fine bark chips or composted leaf mulch that was started with the autumn leaf drop. Throughout summer it will reduce moisture loss on the surface and prevent roots and bulbs being overheated in the sun. The garden will need generous watering in spring to keep soil damp and for plants to become robust. Later in summer a good soaking once a week should maintain plants like these. ❧

GARDEN SUMMARY

aspect at least half a day's sun   **climate** temperate or cool subtropical
soil rich, slow draining, moist   **water** enough to keep soil moist
photographed in spring and summer   **maintenance** medium

---

1 BAY TREES
Laurus nobilis
Dark green leathery leaves make this a dramatic accent plant. It can grow to a large tree 12m high but frequent trimming of stems and leaves (stored for cooking) will help keep it a rounded shrub as seen here. Glossy black berries follow the creamy spring flowers. It grows densely in open sun but can cope with filtered shade.

2 TULIPS
Tulipa varieties
The swan-like heads of tulips are the feature in this scene. Several flower forms have been used and each variety is planted in clusters for maximum

impact. There are double forms and open lily-flowered forms as well as the traditional shape. See page 8 for information on bulb care and planting. They also look spectacular grown in pots, and make fabulous presents. Tulips must be in cold soil to develop. Paper-white jonquils, though less dramatic, could suit milder gardens. Tulips look striking in a vase if you can bear to cut them.

3 TILLANDSIA
Tillandsia xerographica
This plant will actually grow without soil in sphagnum moss or a similar medium. It wintered in its pot, under greenhouse conditions, and is now

of seed to nearby farmland, trim off the flower before seeds develop. Globe artichoke or mullein could substitute.

7 FORGET-ME-NOT
Myosotis alpestris
The white-flowered form is used here. Seedlings planted over the tulip bulbs in late winter/early spring will grow to a flowering tuft 20cm by 20cm by early summer. They become leggy as flowers progress up the stem, and will produce sticky seeds. Trim them to tidy. Seedlings will spring up everywhere.

8 VARIEGATED HONESTY
Lunaria annua 'Variegata'
This white-flowered form has white-edged leaves as well, which lighten the greenery of their corner. Plant seed in semi-shade in early spring. After flowering, its next act follows, the development of flat, green, circular seed heads. These age to silver papery discs, a nice addition to dry winter vases. Honesty will re-seed generously in moist conditions.

9 SOLOMONS SEAL
Polygonatum multiflorum
Soft arching canes almost 1m long grow from this shade- and moisture-loving root stock each spring. Greenish flowers drop from each leaf joint.

10 WORMWOOD
Artemisia 'Valerie Finnis'
Another grey accent with this unusual long but undivided-leafed wormwood. It is not demanding and is best in sun. Trim to tidy.

11 VIBURNUM
There are many cultivars of viburnum, so select one from your nursery that is deciduous, white-flowered and will grow to at least 2m for an effect like this. Flowers are followed by attractive heads of berries and the foliage will later develop good autumn colour. Keep the roots moist and prune to control or shape after flowering. To thin out overcrowded stems, cut old stems at the base and trim top foliage before pulling it away from the plant.

---

displayed in an urn. Its twisted silvery leaves grow from a rosette base. Frost-tolerant ivy or grasses could substitute and these can remain outside during the winter months.

4 PLANTAIN LILY
Hosta crispula
Shade and moisture loving plantain lilies make great impact each spring as their lush crinkled foliage starts to emerge and unfurl. This form has a white edge to its large oval leaves. In summer mauve-white flowers open on spikes above the leaves, but these are relatively insignificant and plantain lilies are grown mainly for their decorative foliage. Beware, snails love them too, so be prepared to deal with them. This plant will be screened from the sun as surrounding foliage develops. Hosta 'Halcyon' has blue-grey foliage and could also suit such a planting.

5 ENGLISH DAISIES
Bellis perennis
This small, button daisy is really a perennial which emerges each spring with a rosette of leaves. Out of these stand budded stems opening to a finely-petalled white flower with a touch of red. A weed of lawns to some and a garden spark to others, it is usually planted in late winter as a spring-flowering annual, placed at garden edges as a low growing accent.

6 SCOTCH THISTLE
Onopordium acanthum
An emblem to the Scots, a weed in warmer climes and a feature plant to gardeners, it is here used in the last mode, making use of its grey-streaked foliage. A small plant so far, the stunning leaves will expand to cover 1m width and the central stem will grow 1.5m high. If trying to stop the spread

WHITE ANNUALS AND PERENNIALS

*A*s the spring display starts to fade, summer flowers emerge. The backdrop is intensely green with bay and viburnum without blossom. Tulip foliage must not be removed but will be obscured by summer annuals and perennials as they grow. Water well to establish, feed with liquid fertiliser every two weeks and mulch around each plant. ∼

PHOTO: LEIGH CLAPP. PICTURED AT GLEDSWOOD, NSW, AUSTRALIA

ANNUALS

POPPIES
Papaver somniferum
Seed of white poppies can be sprinkled over the garden in early spring and seedlings thinned as necessary.

COSMOS
Cosmos bipinnatus 'Purity'
Plant as seed or seedlings, for fine-leafed growth to masses of flowers on tall stems throughout summer.

PETUNIAS
Petunia hybrids
Buy white seedlings or raise from seed and plant at garden edges in spring.

ENGLISH DAISIES
Bellis perennis
These trim the border, with neat upright stems emerging from a flat crown of leaves. They are a perennial but are easier to manage as annual plantings.

PERENNIALS

IRIS
In spring bulbous Dutch iris 'Casa Blanca' shone brightly and in summer *Iris laevigata* 'Alba' follows on, grown from a rhizome under the soil. They like rich moist soil.

VALERIAN
Centranthus 'Alba'
Generously flowering from spring to autumn, this grey-leafed perennial covers bulb foliage as it becomes yellow and dies down. It will move aside as irises emerge. Trim off spent flowers and cut back in autumn.

DAISIES
Argyranthemum frutescens
A shrubby daisy, it will keep flowering through summer if dead flowers are regularly cut off to new bud growth just down the stem. It can survive winter but may be more vigorous if newly planted as a flowering specimen each spring. Strike cuttings in autumn for new plant supplies. Daisies make excellent cut flowers, and cutting them produces more blooms.

PHOTO: LEIGH CLAPP. PICTURED AT GLEDSWOOD, NSW, AUSTRALIA

PHOTO: LEIGH CLAPP. PICTURED AT RED COW FARM, NSW, AUSTRALIA

THE COTTAGE FENCE

The prim white picket fence is given an exuberant overlay with massed plantings on either side. Roses and their thorns have been set against and twined through the palings with passer-by friendly plants filling out the border.

*T*his late spring or early summer view shows a nicely blended arrangement of pinky-red valerian, rock rose and poppies, the lime-yellow of spurge, cream rose blooms with plum-coloured foliage and massed clumps of pink and white seaside daisies to fill in the gaps.

The climate here is temperate, but all the plants used will survive in Mediterranean or cool subtropical zones. Tropical alternatives are suggested.

Soil must be rich but well drained. Use a heavy mulch of manure in autumn or winter when plants are trimmed back or divided. To boost growth in spring and the outset of summer, add complete fertilizer or pelleted slow release poultry manure. Mulch over this with composted fine bark chips or lucerne hay to reduce moisture loss and add more organic matter to the soil. This can be dug in, if worms haven't done it for you, before new mulch is applied. ➣

GARDEN SUMMARY

aspect full sun   **climate** temperate
soil free draining but enriched
water not demanding
photographed in early summer
maintenance medium

1 VALERIAN
Centranthus ruber
This perennial grows from a greyish-leafed clump and its stems reach out in all directions to about 80cm. Panicles of flowers top each stem through the warm months. Trim the stems as the flowers fade to encourage more development. Plant as here at 50cm intervals and cut back to the base in winter in mild areas; early spring in temperate climates. In tropical zones try *Alternanthera ficoidea* cultivars.

2 SEASIDE DAISY
Erigeron karvinskianus
Masses of pink and white tiny daisies stand above this ground-hugging perennial in spring to early winter. Tolerant of most conditions, it does need to be trimmed into place. Try white busy lizzies in tropical areas.

3 SPURGE
Euphorbia sikkimensis
Flowering lime green in late spring, this spreading perennial gives vital contrast.

Cut for vases (soaking the stem ends in boiling water to stop the milky sap) or trim back finished stems to encourage new growth. It grows to 1m by 1m so position as accents where needed.

4 ROCK ROSE
Cistus cultivars
Gleaming open flowers dot the rock rose throughout warm weather, its spreading limbs intertwining through the fence and among its neighbours. It thrives in well drained soil and needs little but tidy up trimming. *Mussaenda alicia* could do tropical duty.

5 POPPY
Papaver somniferum
A cluster of double-petalled pink summer-flowering poppies stand sufficiently tall (almost 1m) from the greyish foliage to be seen in the garden behind. As the petals fall the seed pod enlarges and looks dramatic. They may re-seed but plant new seedlings in late winter just in case. Pink cannas would substitute in the tropics.

6 FLOWERING ONION
Allium cultivars
Long strappy leaves sprout from a cluster of bulbs; long stems topped with an onion dome open out as a cluster of stars in summer, and long lasting seed heads finish the act. White agapanthus could be a substitute (leave the seed heads on) and try red ginger lily in the tropics.

7 ROSES
The cream rose is a climbing form of 'Lady Hillingdon'. An old-fashioned favourite with plum-coloured new foliage and clean tea rose fragrance, it flowers over a long period. Prune stems that go beyond your design. The red is Alister Clark's rose 'Nancy Haywood', another generous flowerer with open single blooms. Both are tolerant of a wide range of conditions. In the tropics vines could substitute and would no doubt cover the fence in no time at all, but clerodendron or bougainvillea could be pruned to control their spread and keep sight of the picket fence.

LET'S LOOK AT YELLOW

Yellow strikes a happy note in a garden scheme but sadly is often avoided. It can be bright and vivacious to startle and attract attention or toned down to a softer cream-yellow which blends with almost every colour grouping.

YELLOW AND PURPLE ▷

Perfect contrasts in flower shape as well as colour, the smooth cream surface of *Achillea* 'Taygetea' acts as a plate upon which is served a spiked presentation of sea holly, *Eryngium bourgatii* 'Oxford Blue'.

◁ **YELLOW AND ORANGE**

An unusual and vibrant combination that will last at least three months, these long stems of yellow kangaroo paws, *Anigozanthos flavidus* variety, grow from their dark green strappy bases among which seed of the feathery-leafed Californian poppy, *Eschscholzia californica*, was planted during winter or early spring. They both enjoy sunny dry conditions.

YELLOW AND RED ▷

Not often paired in isolated splendour like this, yellow and red certainly makes a bright focus. These two thrive in tropical or subtropical conditions. Yellow trumpets of the shrubby allamanda, *Allamanda cathartica*, occur at the end of draping stems allowing it to entwine with the vine *Mussaenda erythrophylla*. On this the flowers are tiny but the bright red bracts are dramatic in winter.

UNDER THE TREES

Attractive trunks can be a garden feature as seen here, with the white mottled bark on this cluster of Silver Birches. Cluster planting produces differing trunk angles and thicknesses, intensifying the impact.

For such informal planting, don't measure distances apart. Position the pots randomly until satisfied or try landscape designer, Edna Walling's technique of throwing a handful of potatoes in the air and planting a tree where each one lands. The dappled sunlit area beneath has been planted with cranesbills and balloon flowers, both enjoying some shade. Pictured in summer with full leaf cover, this temperate garden will translate to cool subtropical or Mediterranean areas as long as water is available to prevent the birches desiccating. Some alternative plantings are suggested to cope with drier or humid conditions. Soil should retain some moisture, enhanced by twice-yearly applications of fine bark mulch. Nutrient levels are maintained by adding pelleted poultry manure under the mulch each time. Trunk beauty can be displayed by a single trunk, an avenue, a grove or formal grid planting. See your nursery for advice on suitable display trees to suit your conditions. ⌒

GARDEN SUMMARY

aspect trees in at least half a day's sun **climate** temperate, Mediterranean or subtropical **soil** well mulched, slow draining
water soak birch in hot or dry spells, once a week for others
photographed in summer **maintenance** low

1 SILVER BIRCH
Betula pendula 'Tristis'
A deciduous tree, renowned for its bark, this cultivar has a smaller crown better suiting a cluster planting like this. Individually they will reach 12m with a 2 or 3m spread. They must have adequate water to prevent crisping and early fall of the leaves. C r e p e Myrtle, *Lagerstroemia indica*, is less

demanding and leopard tree, *Caesalpinia ferea,* would suit subtropical gardens.

2 CRANESBILLS

Geranium species
Not what are usually called geraniums (really pelargoniums) but a soft-stemmed and subtle-flowered perennial with very attractive leaves. Plant about 40cm apart, they will spread and may die back in cold areas in winter. In subtropical areas *Begonia rex* cultivars could be substituted. In drier conditions, coloured leaf pelargoniums could feature.

3 BALLOON FLOWER

Platycodon grandiflorum
A perennial that disappears over winter but its silvery foliage reappears through the mulch each spring. Blue, pink or white star blooms burst open from fascinating balloon buds in summer. In subtropical areas try New Guinea hybrid impatiens and in dry shaded condtions, variegated aspidistra.

Winter and spring bulbs can cover winter bareness.

WATER GARDEN

With beautiful simplicity in the structures — an arched entry, tile-topped wall and terracotta urn — the scene is set for an informal planting around a pond. Upright strappy leaves of iris, libertia and grasses contrast with the roundness of the rocks, the large ligularia leaves and the iris flowers. Even the mass of libertia flowers forms a round of white.

Colouring is green and white to impart coolness, in contrast to the baked wall and sunny brightness beyond. A rose and ivy drape the wall and strappy leaves of iris are repeated here.

The plantings in this courtyard would suit Mediterranean, temperate or subtropical zones as the water feature and walled protection create their own microclimate.

The depression used for a pond must be sited in a "normal" position and not, for example, on a rise. Dig out sufficient depth for pots or fish. Line with pool liner or build with bricks and concrete. Conceal the edges with rocks, some overhanging the pond for frog and fish protection. Keep mosquitoes at bay by introducing purchased native fish, making sure they will be compatible with frog spawn, if you want to offer them a home. It is essential that pond fish will not harm native fish if they are released or escape in floodings, so take care with your selection. A re-circulating pump could fill the urn and allow a gentle cascade down its sides to the pool below.

Arrange the contrasting leaf shapes and flower producers carefully so there will be balance to the scene as they grow. There will have to be frequent trimming back of growth to maintain glimpses of water. ∽

GARDEN SUMMARY

aspect dappled sun **climate** Mediterranean, temperate or subtropical **soil** boggy, rich
water maintain pond level **photographed in** spring **maintenance** low

---

1 LIGULARIA
Ligularia 'Gregynog Gold'
Happy in semi-shade and a moist soil, this perennial has large leaves on long dark stems and yellow spikes of flowers in late summer. It will probably need confining trims.

2 LIBERTIA
Libertia formosa
This evergreen clump-forming perennial has narrow leaves about 50cm long. Stems of frothy white flowers stand above the clump in early spring. They like sun or semi-shade, and moist conditions beside the pond, but will succumb to heavy frosts unless mulched well with straw or leaves. Divide after flowering if necessary.

3 SWEET FLAG
Acornus calamus 'Variegatus'
Cream-streaked sword-like leaves will be pink tinged in spring as they re-emerge from winter dormancy. The leaves smell of mandarin. The plant grows best with at least half a day's sun in bog edge conditions and will develop into a 60cm clump. Trim off ragged foliage in autumn.

4 IRIS
Iris fulva
Bog or Louisiana irises are the ones to grow either in water or in damp conditions at its edge. There are many cultivars, so choose for flower colour and season. They will not survive heavy frost. Use a potted *I. fimbriata* for these conditions, but move it out of the damp for winter.

5 IRIS
Iris foetidissima
This iris flowers later in summer, on branched spikes. The flowers are yellow, or purple and yellow mixes. In autumn its cylindrical seed pods crack open to reveal bright red seeds. At its feet are hardy ferns. For a lovely effect, try growing Arum lilies, *Zantedeschia*, next to irises.

◄ DAHLIA

Showy and bright through summer and autumn, dahlias generously provide flowers for the garden and vase. They grow from tubers, their leaves emerging in spring and their canes growing to 30cm on short varieties and up to 1.5m on tall species. These tall ones need staking to stop the canes breaking under the weight of flowers. Cut for vases and always trim off 1 or 2cm from the stem as they are put in water. Deadhead to encourage new buds to develop. Prune back to ground level once leaves get tatty and lift the tubers to a protected position if frosts are expected.

▼ DAISY

There's a place for these generous flowerers in almost every sunny garden. They will spot flower through winter, cover the plant in colour in spring and continue through summer and autumn. Regularly deadhead daisies and trim back to lower bud clusters when the upper one is finished.

▲ LENTEN ROSE

Evergreen with crisp divided leaves, the lenten rose, *Helleborus*, is a perennial which loves cool to cold conditions and partial shade. It produces arching stems of buds during late autumn which open as nodding bell-shaped, oddly green, purple or whitish flowers in late winter and spring. They can last a couple of months, and are charming and woodsy.

LONG FLOWERING PLANTS

Many plants can feature over a long period, even when not in flower, their leaf shape, colour and form, or their seed cases enduring to make an impact. They are often quite suitable for vase life too. However, in this selection are some of the plants that keep flowering over many months, creating pools of colour in the garden and an abundant supply of material to use in vases.

◀ **BUSY LIZZIE**

Just so useful, busy lizzies, *Impatiens* cultivars, grow in shade or sun, in neat clumps or spreading clusters and flower happily almost all year; select varieties and colours to suit your needs.

▼ **PRINCE OF ORANGE**

The 'Prince of Orange', *Ixora* cultivar, is a tropical shrub that has been extensively modified to give a show of dusky orange or red flowers for most of the year in tropical or subtropical conditions. It looks especially good in pots or in a hedge.

▲ **CANNA**

Cannas bloom from spring to autumn in temperate gardens and into winter in tropical and subtropical climates. The usual colours are orange, yellow, cream and salmon. Lush leaves wrap the base of the flowering stem and are often used as a feature in their own right, being available in rich bronze or cream, streaked with green.

A TROPICAL BORDER

Lush tranquillity and seclusion describe this display.
Low maintenance and ease in replicating the effect are other
assets. The simplicity of this planting is its feature, with
assorted frond-like foliage and occasional points of contrast.
Scaled down or up, it could fit into most garden scenes.

The specimens used here must have frost-free conditions but alternatives could be used in cooler conditions and still maintain the lush ambience. Protection from dry or battering winds, provided here by tall background trees, is essential. Plenty of compost and manure are needed to establish this planting but it will become self sustaining if leaf litter is left undisturbed over time. Watering to establish new planting is essential but can be reduced as the palms develop. The shallow-rooted plants in the front — tree ferns, elephant ears and busy lizzies — will need regular leaf and root moisture.

PHOTO: GEOFFREY BURNIE. PICTURED AT IMPACT PLANT NURSERY, NSW, AUSTRALIA

GARDEN SUMMARY

aspect shade and protection from wind **climate** subtropical
soil enriched but well draining **water** essential to establish palm grove then sufficient to keep border plants lush **photographed in** spring
maintenance low

growing types with slower ones. Plant in unstructured clumps not in neat measured rows, to create the natural effect seen here.

2 TREE FERNS

Cyathea and *Dicksonia* species *Cyathea* are faster growing than *Dicksonia* and usually have a thinner trunk. They will also re-seed themselves in moist spots. *Dicksonia* can clump with new fronds from their base and will tolerate frosts. These are sold as

1 PALMS

A rich assortment have been used here, with differing leaf shapes, trunk details, and original heights at planting time. Ask at your nursery or a palm specialist for what they have in stock and what they can order in to suit your needs. Avoid all one type, but mix fast

variously sized trunks. They both need moisture to get established and fronds will shrivel in hot dry conditions so plant with shade protection and give the foliage moisture sprays when conditions are very dry. Trim off dead lower fronds to keep the palm neat and lush looking.

3 ELEPHANT EARS
Alocasia varieties
Plant purchased specimens or root divisions from generous friends. They grow from large tufted rhizomes and will multiply rapidly. Keep them watered and note how they bow down to say "thank you" as you wet them. *Gunnera* could substitute in frosty areas.

4 RED IVY
Hemigraphis alternata
This dramatic purple-black plant is a fabulous contrast among the green. It spreads to 1.5m round and will need maintenance trims. Purple-leafed, *Philodendron erubescens*, growing up a palm, has long red stalks, and the lustrous coppery sheen on its dark green leaves repeats this contrast. In cool areas purple *Dracaena* would make a good substitute.

5 BUSY LIZZIE
Impatiens cultivars
Shade-loving busy lizzies spot flower in pink and purple tones. Just take care they don't become dominant; they seed themselves readily. Weed out any in colours you don't want.

THE ROMANTIC GARDEN

*An archway, abundantly rose-dressed, frames the entry
to a circular brick pathway with a seat and a central
bird bath enclosed by flowers and aromatic leaves.
The result, a romantic secluded hideaway
filled with scented air.*

There are neighbours and a street nearby, but they don't intrude on the private haven of this gardener. The picture was taken in spring with that generous burst of bloom that denotes warmer air and increased sunlight. Full sun now will become dappled shade by late afternoon as trees and the house block the westering sun.

The soil is rich and slow draining, liberally laced with pelleted poultry manure and deeply mulched before each planting season. Regular watering in spring will get seed to sprout, seedlings to develop and perennials to become bushy. Once established, a long soaking once a week will keep all happy. Don't rely on rain sprinkles. 🙝

PHOTO: LEIGH CLAPP. DESIGNED BY JUDY ANDREWS, NSW, AUSTRALIA

GARDEN SUMMARY

aspect at least half a day's full sun **climate** temperate, Mediterranean or subtropical
soil slow draining, well mulched and fertilised **water** to get seedlings established
in spring; to soak the rose roots **photographed in** spring **maintenance** high

---

ROSES

1 *Rosa* 'Cymbeline'
The large floppy dusty-pink blooms of this rose are very fragrant and are produced over a long period.

2 *Rosa* 'Honeyflow'
Sweetly honey scented, this rose produces huge sprays of clustered single white flowers opening from rich pink buds. It is a robust grower.

3 *Rosa* 'Carabella'
Similar to 'Honeyflow' but a bit pinker and just as generous with its flowers. These two make a fine rosy mass. Trim off spent flower heads to encourage new buds, but from late summer leave some of them on so hips will develop as a winter feature.

All these roses cope with humidity, but are always best in dry summers with a cool to cold winter. As scrambling roses, they don't need heavy pruning, only enough to keep them shapely and to allow access without thorn arrest.

4 WORMWOOD
Artemisia 'Powis Castle'
A foaming wave a grey foliage from this cultivar surrounds the bird bath.

10 FOXGLOVES
Digitalis purpurea
This is really a short-lived perennial, surviving only two seasons. Plant new seedlings in semi-shaded positions in autumn and mulch to protect if necessary, for spring flowers. In cool temperate areas they will self-seed.

11 CHINESE FORGET-ME-NOT
Cynoglossum amabile
An annual that actually re-seeds itself generously. Tuck them into bare patches as needed in late winter and you'll have them for life.

12 PINKS
Dianthus x *allwoodii*
Evergreen (but really grey) tufted foliage produces pinkish-toned cinnamon-scented flowers throughout the warm months. Trim off scraggly edges.

13 CRANESBILLS
Geranium varieties
Attractive foliage and soft lanky growth distinguish these real geraniums from the tougher stemmed plants, most usually so-called. Cranesbills produce gentle clusters of flowers in purple-pink tones in spring and summer.

14 EVENING PRIMROSE
Oenothera speciosa
This low spreading perennial has pale pink flowers shaped like small cups during spring and summer. Plant in early spring and trim back lightly after flowering. They may need replacing every few years, being less than robust, as their delicate appearance suggests.

15 LAMIUM
Lamium 'White Nancy'
White-mottled green leaves on this ground cover bring light to the shade, wherein this plant thrives. In summer it has white flowers.

16 ARISTEA
Aristea major
A strappy-leafed clump which sends up tall spikes of rich blue flowers in summer, much the colour of Chinese forget-me-not.

Tolerant of most conditions and soils, its only needs are good sun and a gentle trim to keep it from overflowing. Plant potted specimens 30cm apart.

5 ROSE CAMPION
Lychnis coronaria
More grey, but this time from rosettes of leaves close to the ground which send up 30cm tall velvety spikes. These open as rose-red flat flower heads that love to intermingle with other flowering stems. Pick for the vase, to encourage more blooms and fewer seedlings.

6 WILD IRIS
Dietes grandiflora
This perennial has strappy leaves about 1m long. In spring a flush of iris-like flowers, coloured white and mauve appear on taller stems, continuing spasmodically through summer. The clump will expand and may need dividing eventually in early winter.

7 CRAB APPLE
Malus ioensis 'Plena'
This double-flowering shrub is part of the screening border. It is deciduous, developing some colour in autumn and usually sprouts a few new spring leaves before the cluster blossoms open. It produces no fruit.

8 TOBACCO FLOWER
Nicotiana cultivars
Seen here as deeply pink, they are planted each side of the seat so their soft perfume can be appreciated. Plant two or three seedlings in a cluster to make an impact, in a sunny position, by late winter to early spring after frosts.

9 POPPIES
Papaver rhoeas Shirley series
Sow in seed punnets in early winter with protection if necessary, and transplant as required. Hairy stems emerge with downcast buds that lift as they open in soft pink or red colours.

ROSES

Just as there are "horses for courses", there are roses for poses. Almost everyone wants one or some in their gardens, but the key to success is to select the ones that will grow in your environment, that will produce the effect you want and that appeal to you. It may need some research (books on roses are numerous), observation of what performs well in your area and care with initial placing and planting for a rosy result, but they are certainly worth the effort. Unhealthy looking plants are a miserable sight, don't let it happen in your quest for a rose. The photographs below demonstrate rose poses not rose varieties.

MASSED VARIETIES ▶

Every rose fancier's dream, the full mixed panoply of massed blooms, a swathe of petal-strewn lawn and an assortment of healthy and varied plants. A lot of work goes into such a display but nature helps if conditions are right. It's a team effort.

▼ **COUNTRY STYLE**

Draping itself over the outhouse in wonderful country style is the rambler rose 'Dorothy Perkins'. Its leaves can become troubled with mildew, and its perfume is not as abundant as its blooms, so select the rambler of colour and variety to suit your conditions.

◀ **PICKET FENCE**

A rose twining through a fence is useful, traditional and attractive. This is an Australian rose, 'Lorraine Lee', bred for local conditions, flowering almost all year and delightfully perfumed. Take care that its thorns don't poke through the fence and attack passers-by.

IN POTS ▶

Growing in a pot is an abundant 'Carabella', with its clusters of pink and cream single blooms that repeat generously if trimmed off regularly. Towards the end of summer, leave some blooms on the bush, as attractive hips develop to complete the display. Feed and water pot- grown roses generously. At its feet is a *Helichrysum petiolare*.

SILVER
SPLENDOUR

These three plants, massed together in a Mediterranean garden produce a bold silvery-grey statement in a sunny border.

The plants will survive both temperate and subtropical conditions as well. They could easily cover an area 5m by 5m, and none of them is demanding of water, rich soil or protection from pests. They will need constant trimming to control their spreading ways and, in the case of the butterfly bush, to encourage more flowers.

GARDEN SUMMARY

aspect full sun   **climate** Mediterranean   **soil** fast draining
watering occasional soak to prevent wilting   **photographed in** summer
maintenance medium

1 DUSTY MILLER
Senecio viravira
A very generous grower, this dusty miller, true to its name is liberally dusted with flour all over, making it gleamingly whitish-silver. Yellow buttons of flowers appear in summer. Plant a single plant in early spring in cool areas, any time where it's milder, and it will easily spread to 2m. Regular trimmings will keep it producing fresh floury leaves.

2 HELICHRYSUM
Helichrysum petiolare
This helichrysum has round grey leaves on reaching grey stems. It smells of curry when bruised but the fine-leafed helichrysum is the one called curry bush. The long stems need regular trimming control as the bush is unsightly when pruned back hard. However, it will recover. Flat greyish-cream flower heads appear later in summer. The leaves and flowers, both fresh and dried, look good in vases.

3 BUTTERFLY BUSH
Buddleia davidii 'White Bouquet'
Forming a dense background, this white-flowered, velvety-leaved buddleia has a tendency to become straggly, but compact dense foliage is possible if it receives a good pruning back in late autumn or early spring. Flowers are honey-scented and nectar-rich and are loved by honeyeaters and bees as well as butterflies.

PHOTO: LEIGH CLAPP

PHOTO: LEIGH CLAPP. PICTURED AT BAREWOOD, NEW ZEALAND.

THE VEGETABLE AND HERB GARDEN

This abundant kitchen garden is decorative and productive. Herbs, fruit trees, vegetables and cutting flowers all have a place in this sun-baked area close to the house. Fruit trees are centred in each square bed with a central bay tree circled by thyme, violas and nasturtiums. Paths provide access.

This garden is in a temperate zone, but many of these plants can adapt to Mediterranean or cool subtropical conditions. The idea of the garden is that it should be productive but also attractive to gaze upon and walk through. There are no regimented rows of vegetables, everything is mixed together with an appealing casualness, but there is a plan behind the apparent randomness. It is essential when planting nitrogen-greedy vegetables to position different varieties in a new spot each year, so bean types will follow leaf crops followed by root crops etc. This means the nutrients used by one crop will be replaced by the next. It also results in fewer attacks by insects and diseases.

Soil should be richly fertilised, well laced with organic matter to slow down moisture loss, and traditionally, well dug. Lucerne hay or leaf mulch applied twice a year will suppress weeds, maintain moisture and lighten the soil. Plant only what you need and what can grow happily in your climate. Whimsical details like the dovecote here give added charm. ∾

GARDEN SUMMARY

aspect full sun **climate** temperate **soil** slow draining, well fed **water** every 2 days for vegetables
photographed in early summer **maintenance** high

1 ENGLISH LAVENDER

Lavandula angustifolia

Try 'Munstead Dwarf' or 'Hidcote Blue' for a nice low border like this. Plant 80cm to 1m apart in autumn. Cut summer flowers as needed for vases or dry for potpourri, lavender bags and infusions. Trim off remaining stalks and stem growth by half after flowering is finished, to maintain round shape.

2 BORAGE

Borago officinalis

Large-leafed borage produces the softer mauve flowers behind the lavender. Plant seed in late winter, under protection if necessary, and transplant at 50cm intervals. Star-like flowers twinkle in summer and are edible. They re-seed liberally, so pull up tatty plants in autumn, and move the seedlings to next year's position.

3 LUPINS

Lupinus varieties

Pretty and practical, the flowers look good and the roots add nitrogen to the soil. Plant seed where needed in spring and dig plants into the soil when finished, saving seed for replanting.

4 FENNEL

Foeniculum vulgare

A seedling of fennel planted in early spring will produce flowers by summer but will need a few years to clump as here. The soft, feathery leaves topped by lime yellow flowers and seed make it an attractive and useful vegetable. The flavour and aroma is of aniseed.

5 SUNFLOWER

Helianthus annuus

A whimsical giant in this garden, large stem, huge leaves and a massive "sun" on top in summer. Plant seed in early spring in feature spots.

6 CURRANTS

Ribes varieties

A fruiting shrub for cool, moist gardens, it will grow approximately 2m by 2m. Grow from a cutting or buy a variety that does well in your area. A couple of plants, at least 2m apart, will produce plenty of fruit for jams and desserts.

7 ASPARAGUS

Asparagus officinalis

Deep, rich soil, ample moisture and lots of mulching of several "crowns" will produce a crop each spring in a year or two after planting. Always leave a few stems to keep the plant going. Prune off before spring and mulch deeply.

8 BAY

Laurus nobilis

Here a young specimen that is destined for a round tufted head takes centre stage. It can grow to 12m, so don't plant it here if not planning to trim.

9 GOLDEN HOPS

Humulus lupulus 'Aureus'

Tripods hold early growth of golden hops, a twining climber.

Surrounding beds grow lettuces, onions, tomatoes in fact all that the chef requires from the kitchen garden.

FOCUSING ON PINK

Many people love pink in their gardens, and many flowers obligingly have beautiful pink forms. However the colours they are combined with can make or break the display. Here are some pleasing groupings.

PINK, WHITE AND LIME ▶

Pink at its softest in roses; select several of one variety that suits your needs and garden conditions. Plant with some white forms for contrast and fill in the spaces with white and pink cottage plants like spires of foxgloves, clumps of columbines, valerian and white low-growing *Gladiolus* 'The Bride'. The sharpness of limey yellow spurge completes this late spring scene.

◀ PINK AND WHITE

Toning down the hot pink of these 'Carmine Glow' primulas is the pure white form teamed with another white with a central splotch of the same pink — this is a fairly new hybrid. The planter edges are softened by alyssum clumps. In a sunny protected position this display will provide colour from winter to spring.

◀ PINK, PURPLE OR ORANGE

Providing its own contrasting colour brighteners are the tan flowers on the same flower head as the musk pink on this perennial wallflower. There are several different colour groupings in these pink-toned forms, some mauve to purple, others tan-orange, so take care when selecting what it is to team with. Prune back hard in early summer for flowers the following winter and spring.

PINK AND PINK ▶

The rich tones of mandevilla, a summer-flowering non-aggressive twiner have been teamed with the autumn-flowering deeper pink spider lily, *Lycoris squamigera*, providing flower shape and colour enrichment. Pale pink-toned alyssum could be planted at their feet for a summer-long addition.

FRAMING STEPS

These neatly constructed steps are exuberantly dressed by undemanding sun-loving plants. Each is interwoven generously with its partners, linking the levels of this climbing display. This scene is possible in Mediterranean, temperate or subtropical zones, in gardens enjoying full sun.

Soil on built up terraces or a slope will usually be fast draining, and needs quantities of mulch to reduce moisture loss. Apply garden or spent mushroom compost or cow manure twice a year and cover this with fine bark mulch. Add complete plant food or pelleted poultry manure under the compost in early spring. All these plants enjoy a sunbaked position but like a good soaking during dry spells. Maintenance includes trimming of spent blooms and trailing stems.

GARDEN SUMMARY

aspect full sun   **climate** temperate, subtropical or Mediterranean
soil well drained but well mulched   **water** soak in extended dry periods
photographed in spring   **maintenance** low

---

1 POPPY
Papaver rhoeas Shirley series
Plant seed in autumn and transplant seedlings in late winter for red, pink or watercolour mixes in spring. Buds lift their lowered heads to open.

2 GAURA
Gaura lindheimeri
When poppies are finished and pulled out, the gaura will take over. Fine stems with delicate white-tinged pink flowers stand nearly 1m high. Trim all off at the end of flowering, mulch and feed the clump.

3 CRANESBILL
Geranium cultivar
A real geranium with soft stems and deeply toothed, divided leaves (seen wandering onto the path) flowers intense blue in spring and summer. It will form a clump that can be divided and it will seed itself.

4 CHINESE FORGET-ME-NOT
Cynoglossum amabile
Both blue and white flowering forms seen here grow from a grey-green-leafed annual that will re-seed itself generously. Bees will cross pollinate the two varieties so seedlings will be variably coloured. For only one colour remove the alternative as soon as the buds open. Plant seedlings at 30cm intervals to allow for bulky growth.

5 MULLEIN
Verbascum olympicum
Large hairy silvery leaves lying flat on the soil will send spires 2m high with tightly packed yellow flowers in summer. It can re-seed.

6 WILD IRIS
Dietes grandiflora
The strappy leaves here produce stems and buds, opening white and mauve with a streak of yellow. After a spring flush, flowers continue into autumn.

7 DAYLILIES
Hemerocallis cultivars
Daylilies true to name, last only a day, but are followed by a succession of buds on the emergent stalks. Green strappy leaves may remain all year or die down in winter, depending on the cultivar selected. Flowers appear at intervals throughout the warm months.

8 ROCK ROSE
Cistus cultivar
This pure white form with crinkled, leathery leaves has long spreading branches. Trim only lightly as it won't regrow from woody stems.

9 PRIDE OF MADEIRA
Echium candicans
An evergreen shrub, growing 1.5 by 1.5m, *Euchium* will become a mass of mauve flowers in summer that age to the green pineapple forms seen here.

10 ROSES
The climber has its great stems contained behind and is topped by soft pink blooms. Try *Rosa* 'Albertine' or *R.* 'Cornelia'. A shrub rose repeats the pink of the daylilies. Try *R.* 'Duchesse de Brabant', happy in dry conditions.

INDEX

WORLD CLIMATE ZONES

Use this map to locate areas of the world with a climate similar to your own. Plants from those regions are most likely to be successful in your garden.

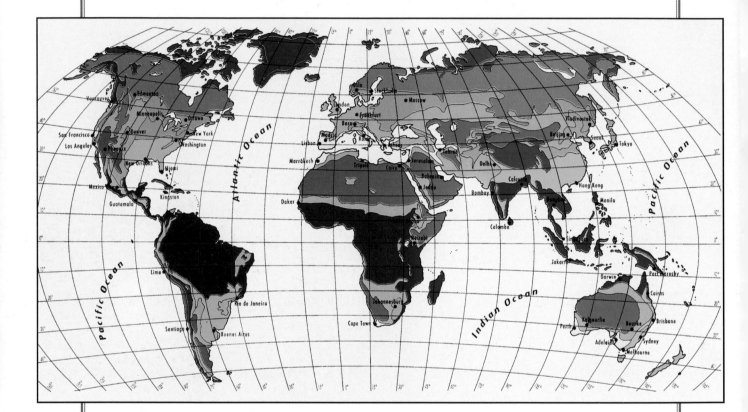

TUNDRA Average summer temperature 0 – 10°C (32 – 50°F). Very severe winters.

SUB-ARCTIC Severe winters. Average temperature above 10°C (50°F) for less than four months.

COLD CONTINENTAL Rain year-round or dry winters. Average summer temperatures below 22°C (72°F).

COOL CONTINENTAL Severe winters but warm to hot summers. Average summer temperature 27°C (80°F). May be rainy year-round or dry in winter.

TEMPERATE Cool winters, warm summers. Average summer temperature 16°C (60°F). May be rainy year-round or wet in winter.

SUBTROPICAL Cool to mild winters, warm to hot summers. Average summer temperature 27°C (80°F). May be rainy year-round or dry in winter.

MEDITERRANEAN Cool to mild winters, warm to hot summers. Average summer temperature 27°C (80°F). Summers dry.

SEMI-ARID PLAINS Seasonal or evenly spread low rainfall. Average summer temperature 32°C (90°F). Cold or mild winters.

DESERT Very low rainfall. Average summer temperature 38°C (100°F). Winters may be cold or mild.

TROPICAL Year-round warmth. High humidity, high rainfall, heaviest in summer; winters may be dry or less wet. Average summer temperature 27°C (80°F).